T0270056

Advance Praise for

Navy Dog

"*Navy Dog: A Dog's Days in the US Navy* is the fun, fascinating, and touching biography of Jenna, a bona fide, four-legged sea dog. Rescued from a dog pound in Japan, Jenna becomes more than a mascot to the crew of the USS *Vandegrift*, she becomes a beloved, inspirational, and full-fledged member of the crew. It's a tale of a lifetime told with warmth and poignancy that will have you laughing at the antics, fill you with rage over the idiocy of desk-bound bureaucrats, and pull at your heart-strings. Well done!"

— DWIGHT JON ZIMMERMAN, *New York Times* bestselling writer and president of the Military Writers Society of America

"A surprising feel good book that is both entertaining, informative, and at times, even humorous. Thoroughly enjoyed it from the first chapter to the end. Written so even us non-Navy guys can understand. A five-star reading experience on any rating chart! I totally endorse and recommend this book knowing that many will truly find it a real treasure."

— REV. BILL MCDONALD, founder of the Military Writers Society of America and the American Authors Association, author, Vietnam War veteran, international motivational speaker, award-winning poet, documentary film advisor, and minister

"Throughout our intersecting careers, both in and after the Navy, I have admired the leadership and tenacity of Captain Neal Kusumoto. *Navy Dog* is yet another aspect of his ability to create a positive command atmosphere through bonding love of his ship's dog, Seaman Jenna, to ensure both his ship and Sailors reached their potential. A 'must read' for anyone who has, or aspires to, 'go down to the sea in ships.'"
— REAR ADMIRAL STEVE LOEFFLER, , U.S. Navy, retired

"Kudos to Neal Kusumoto! In *Navy Dog,* he has woven the improbable and heartwarming tale of Jenna, a canine mascot, aboard a Navy ship and the life of sailors both at sea and in port. A great read!"
— JOHN H. DALTON, 70th Secretary of the Navy

"I can't remember the last book I read that I enjoyed more than this one. I laughed, I cried, I fell in love with Jenna—just as the men of the USS *Vandegrift* did. Not only will you learn about a great dog, but Neal's ability to weave in the everyday workings aboard a Navy ship puts you right up on the Captain's chair with him and Jenna. A great read and a wonderful tale! Bravo, Neal!"
— ROBIN HUTTON, *New York Times* bestselling author of *Sgt. Reckless: America's War Horse* and *War Animals: The Unsung Heroes of World War II*

NAVY DOG

A DOG'S DAYS IN THE US NAVY

NEAL J. KUSUMOTO
CAPTAIN, US NAVY (RET)

KNOX PRESS

A KNOX PRESS BOOK
An Imprint of Permuted Press
ISBN: 978-1-63758-773-7
ISBN (eBook): 978-1-63758-774-4

Navy Dog:
A Dog's Days in the US Navy
© 2023 by Neal J. Kusumoto, Captain, US Navy (ret)
All Rights Reserved

Cover art by Cody Corcoran

This is a work of nonfiction. All people, locations, events, and situation are portrayed to the best of the author's memory.

Permuted Press, LLC
New York • Nashville
permutedpress.com

Published in the United States of America
1 2 3 4 5 6 7 8 9 10

To the Sailors of the United States Navy, who right now are working in dirty bilges and standing watch representing the Stars and Stripes around the world. Because of their sacrifices and hard-won reputation as elite sea warriors, you and I live in peace and safety.

Eternal Father, Strong to save,

Whose arm hath bound the restless wave,

Who bid'st the mighty Ocean deep

Its own appointed limits keep;

O hear us when we cry to thee,

for those in peril on the sea.

—Navy Hymn

CONTENTS

JENNA'S VOYAGE TIMELINE

1984	USS *Vandegrift* commissioned
Oct. 13, 1996 (est.)	Jenna born
Feb. 23–Mar. 23, 1998	*Vandegrift* transits from San Diego to Japan
Apr. 10	Jenna adopted, embarks *Vandegrift*
May	Jenna banned from the fleet
June 19–Aug. 10	RIMPAC exercise (Hawaii)
Oct. 26–Nov. 1	Foal Eagle exercise (Sea of Japan)
Dec. 4–8	Shanghai port visit
Apr. 3, 1999	Chief of Naval Operations visits *Vandy*
May 26	*Vandegrift* crosses the equator (105.30 degrees longitude)
June	Jenna quarantined in Australia
Aug. 2003	Jenna detaches from *Vandegrift*
July 2005	Jenna transfers to Naval Station Ingleside, TX

NEAL J. KUSUMOTO, CAPTAIN, US NAVY (RET)

Apr. 10, 2007	Jenna returns to Kusumoto crew
Oct. 2009	Jenna moves to San Diego
Oct. 13, 2012	Sweet 16 birthday party
Feb. 5, 2013	Jenna passes away
Feb. 19, 2015	USS *Vandegrift* decommissioned

SEAMAN JENNA'S PORT VISITS

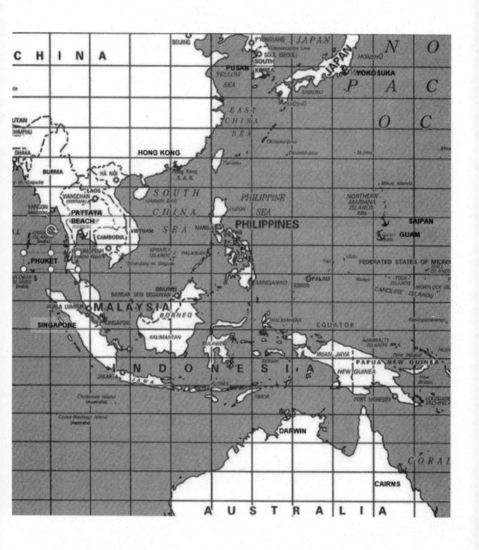

SEAMAN JENNA

A NO-SHITTER (NAVY TERMINOLOGY FOR "NON-FICTION")

To this day sailors still whisper of Seaman Jenna, her unforgettable and outrageous legend one of the most improbable chapters in the US Navy's long history. When I met Jenna, I could never have imagined that she would change the lives of hundreds of sailors and even the course of a Navy warship. That she would become a legend so beloved that even an Admiral could not deep-six her. When Jenna met me, she could not have dreamed that I would enlist her for five years of military service on a steel ship. That she would travel between the hemispheres, across the wide Pacific, through angry seas and becalmed waters. That she would provide joy and comfort to 225 men hardened by grinding ship's work and half-year separations from their families.

Seaman Jenna Vandegrift, US Navy, rose from an orphan scavenging in back alleys to become an icon loved by deck-plate sailors. She was one of thousands of unsung heroes in the Navy, yet became famous despite every attempt to keep a low profile. Her very presence threatened a three-star Admiral, who ordered that she be banished from the naval service. Yet Jenna somehow survived and served for five years on USS *Vandegrift*, a frigate forward deployed in Japan. She was the sole female and only foreign national on that ship and became the center of attention as soon as she set foot on board.

And Jenna was a *dog*.

She was the only canine to become a permanent member of a Navy crew since World War II. We shanghaied Jenna from an animal shelter in Japan and, breaking Navy protocol, impressed her on board, where she captured the hearts of 225 sailors.

This is also the story of a crew forced to leave family and friends, yet overcoming countless obstacles to reach the pinnacle of success. A story highlighting the sacrifices that sailors make for their country, the grueling and foul tasks they perform daily, and the families they leave behind for six months at a time. And how one dog made a difference in all their lives.

This is a story about the Navy's profound impact around the world and how one crew strove to become the best ship in the Navy while also having the most fun allowed by law. We proved ourselves during the largest naval exercise on the planet by sinking three ships and a submarine and shooting two jets out of the sky. Through it all, Jenna, a symbol of individuality within a vast Navy ruled by regulations and strict conformity, kept us smiling and human.

Jenna was a princess warrior on an all-male ship. She got her way no matter what the captain or anyone else proclaimed. Somehow, some way, she pawed her way into our hearts. She was proud; we were proud. She toured the ship daily, touching base with crew members—especially those who sneaked food to her—and bringing a sense of home to a steel-gray ship of iron men. Jenna made *Vandegrift* distinctive among the other three hundred ships within the Navy bureaucracy. No other ship had a dog on board, and there was no record of a dog having lived on a Navy ship in the last forty years.

Jenna became famous, and we basked in her glamorous glow. She was often spotted walking around the naval base escorted by a sailor in his white crackerjack uniform or proudly riding in the passenger seat of the ship's van. Jenna became the figurehead of the *Vandegrift*, and her presence embossed a unique brand that made the ship stick out in an organization that required conformity. In a sense, though not planned, we were thumbing our collective nose at higher authority. And higher authority, in the form of a powerful Admiral, would take notice and strike back. Even the Chief of the Navy—the Navy's top dog—would be drawn into the furry drama.

The stories you are about to read, *sea stories* if you will, are true. *No-shitters* in Navy parlance. If there is something described that was against the law or regulations...let's assume that part was fabricated to enhance the story.

I am proud to say I was the captain of that fine ship, blessed with a magnificent crew that included one special sea dog.

1.

OUTLANDISH PROPOSAL

*If it's a good idea, go ahead and do it.
It's much easier to apologize than
it is to get permission.*

—REAR ADMIRAL GRACE HOPPER, computer pioneer

Ensign LaPointe emphatically stated that he *did not like the Navy.*

My spoon stopped halfway to my mouth, and I slowly raised my head to meet his eyes. What did this very junior officer mean by this shocking remark? He explained that an unmarried sailor couldn't have a dog because when he deploys, the dog must stay with someone else...and when he returns the dog loves that someone else.

I wondered, out loud, whether he was really talking about a dog.

The officers were eating lunch in the wardroom, which is both a formal dining room with traditions and rules as well as the only space for officers to relax during off hours. On our frigate the wardroom was not large, about twenty by twenty feet, most of the space taken up by two long rectangular tables—welded to the deck— surrounded by eighteen chairs. Not a lot of room left for the "relaxing" area, which included a twenty-four-inch TV (no satellite or wireless), an elder stereo that was never plugged in, and a wraparound couch that comfortably seated six but often held ten. Like the rest of the ship, this space was sparse and gray, the only exceptions being the blue rubberized tablecloths and one small porthole that let us peek outside.

"Wardroom" is also a collective term for all the officers assigned to a ship. To say, "Lieutenant Kesselring is in the wardroom" refers to the space, while "Lieutenant Kesselring and the rest of the fuckin' Wardroom are going to conduct an inspection" refers to the group of officers. Every Wardroom has a different personality. Some are formal, with officers standing at attention in front of assigned seats when the captain arrives and professional discussions the norm. I preferred a relaxed Wardroom due to my Hawaiian roots and forbade discussion of work at the table except for the inevitable critique of the food. Talk could turn in any direction, with verbal shots fired at will.

The captain's seat—my seat—was at the head of the larger table, backed to the bulkhead to be able to see everyone. The Executive Officer (XO) was seated to my left and the Department Heads, next in seniority, filled in the nearest seats. The other designated places at my table were for the most junior officer, so he could receive proper "mentoring," and the Food Services Officer, so he could receive immediate feedback on the meal.

In this case, the junior officer requiring guidance (JORG, pronounced "George") was Ensign Matt LaPointe, who had just graduated from the Naval Academy. Standing six foot two and weighing in at a muscular 235 pounds, he was full of fun, leaning forward to take on any challenge. And like most Naval Academy graduates, already sporting a cynical attitude worthy of an old salt. Ensign Nate Johnston, who had played football at the Naval Academy, was the Food Services Officer. Nate displayed a mixture of quiet enthusiasm, uncertainty of his love for the Navy, and a smooth southern wit.

The mascot dialogue became a mainstay at every meal, gaining momentum and taking on a life of its own. Mascots had been a tradition on Navy ships for more than a hundred years, but no ship had embarked a dog since World War II. Mascots in today's Navy are confined to lizards, goldfish, or usually no mascot at all. I soon discovered the ensigns' hidden agenda. The USS *Cushing* was also moving to Japan, and their commanding officer was a good friend of mine. During special evolutions he made an ensign wear a sweltering lion outfit and prance about the outside decks to amuse the crew. This was not an attractive image for my young warfighters, so we took advantage of their discomfort by discussing a wide range of flamboyant options for doing something similar. Or worse.

The ensigns had learned the military art of diversion. They believed a dog would take the place of an ensign wearing a hot, embarrassing costume in public. The topic waxed and waned for weeks. We recognized it as one of those ideas that was fun to kick around... but it was just talk. No Navy ship had maintained a dog onboard since the forties.

A dog on a Navy ship would be impossible.

2.

WEST TO JAPAN

The sailor's life is at the best a life of danger.
He pursues honor on the mountain wave
and finds it in the battle and in the storm.

—President John Tyler

eavy seas slammed into the hull, sending a hollow explosive echo and shudder through the entire ship. With every strike the sound wave outpaced the saltwater wave's physical motion as it traversed our 447-foot frigate. That gave us a microsecond warning to *grab hold of something*. The bow rose with each new swell, reaching an unlikely forty-degree angle pointed toward the leaden sky...pausing dramatically... then crashing down on the back of the next massive wave. Green water trimmed with white foam cascaded over the bow, smearing heavy spray across the bridge windshields. We were battling sustained winds of forty knots (forty-five miles per hour) and twenty-five to thirty-foot waves, which was defined as Sea State 5 out of a possible 9.

On the bridge we weren't deliberating about science or wavelengths...sound velocity...the Beaufort Sea State Scale...or even why we drew a rare and dangerous Santa Ana storm. Even the hot topic of a dog evaporated as we gripped the nearest handhold and wondered how much longer the ship's hull could endure this battering. We had plastic barf bags sticking out of our back pockets that we could quick-draw while still focusing on our jobs. Vomit is its own virus, the curdled smell of warm retch quickly provoking a liquefied chain reaction.

Vandegrift was en route from San Diego to her new home in Japan, and we were having a rough start. Already depressed about leaving families behind, and uncertain about what life would be like overseas, struggling against three-story waves was not what the crew needed. At meals we stuffed down food with one hand while holding onto the table and plates and silverware and cups with the other. We timed our bites to the few calm seconds when the ship was in the trough of each wave, letting go of the table just long enough to smash some food into our mouths then slosh a drink before we roller-coastered into the next titanic wave. It was our version of a Nathan's hot dog eating contest, but with flying silverware.

After days of holding fast to anything solid, fanatically clinging like a cat avoiding a bath, we finally got past the storm. I had been in serious blows during my seventeen years in the Navy, but this was worse than any hurricane. So rough that the waves ripped a hole in the sonar, requiring the ship to enter dry dock in Pearl Harbor for repairs. Despite this violent start to our long voyage, the "good idea" to get a dog mascot quickly spread throughout the ship. The argument for a live-in dog was unmistakably hopeless, yet the happy buzz continued.

Nobody admitted to missing the warmth and comfort of home, but during elongated separations we missed our families' lives, what should have been *our* lives. We were not there for weddings, divorces, deaths, or births. Only a handful of our families were moving to Japan. The majority stayed in San Diego, separated in time and space from their husbands and fathers. The few families that moved weren't allowed to bring their dogs or cats, as rental properties did not allow pets. Pets, dogs in particular, have a special—almost magical—method to unlock human hearts and release pent up angst. The ensigns soon pegged me as a dog lover, and the talk shifted from fanciful to practical.

The question soon changed from "Why should we?" to "Why can't we?"

Based on the Navy bureaucratic storm ahead, the question I should have considered was "Why *shouldn't* we?"

A triad made up of the Commanding Officer (CO), Executive Officer (XO), and Command Master Chief (CMC) leads every Navy ship. Although not a panel or democracy by any means, a good captain involves his two most-trusted advisers on significant decisions. My Executive Officer, second in command, was Lieutenant Commander Steve Sloan. Steve and I had served together on a previous ship. A six-foot-four giant whose broad Frankensteinian shoulders filled the doorway, he swayed on feet too small to support his frame. He loved golf, but his real passion was to serenade every bar in the Western Hemisphere with his distinctive rendering of "The House of the Rising Sun." What luck to have someone so talented and experienced, whom I already trusted, as my primary adviser.

The third member of the *Vandy* triad was Master Chief Mike Ford. Mike was the senior enlisted on board, with more than twenty years of service, and my primary adviser on all things related to the crew. The CMC has great stature based on his proven leadership and extensive sea time. He is charged with ensuring we take care of our young enlisted and preventing the captain from doing something stupid. Again, I was blessed with a great chief who blended old-school, no-nonsense traditions with parental-level concern for the crew. Master Chief was a five-foot-six spark plug with a graying crew cut and mustache. His blue eyes could go from twinkling to you-are-in-big-shit in a nanosecond. Mike was—*is*—as loyal as any human being and still checks up on me today. I trusted Mike implicitly. If he said the sky would be green tomorrow, I got my camera ready for a unique shot.

If you are not a Navy veteran, you might think that the officers run the ship. While technically true, the chief petty officers are the deck-plate leaders who make things happen. Mike got wind of the dog "good idea" and brought it up at our daily meeting in my cabin. I can't remember his exact words, but when he realized that I was considering the idea, "You Can't Be Fuckin' Serious" summed up his point of view. His deck-plate analysis, which did not require graphs or PowerPoint slides, was, "We will be the laughingstock of the Navy!" The XO, who was still riding the fence, remained silent but couldn't contain a big grin.

This put a crimp in things. When the Master Chief expresses a strong opinion, you better listen or be prepared to document a lesson learned. After one spirited discussion, I asked Master Chief to investigate whether there were any rules or regulations prohibiting a dog from living on board a Navy ship. I gave him two weeks. He left with a knowing smirk and confident gait. Surely there must be something in the stacks of regulations amassed over two hundred-plus years that forbade this.

The Wardroom debate continued unabated, gaining strength as we approached the Land of the Rising Sun.

Nothing.

Despite giving the chiefs more time to research, even after we reached Japan, they found nothing that forbade having a dog on board—other than common sense, in their view. Their fresh argument: a dog would stain the ship as a sideshow rather than a lethal warship. I was constantly emphasizing "warfighting first," and they exploited that argument. None of the old salts had ever seen a dog aboard a ship—that could not be a coincidence.

I did love dogs, but I did not want to become part of *McHale's Navy*. With the home port change I got a new boss, Commodore Jerry Ferguson. We were the unproven ship in his squadron of proven winners, and it would take time to prove ourselves in Japan. We didn't need a distraction.

In retrospect, I also disregarded what a canine tattoo on my service record might do to my career.

The commodore and his wife turned out to be dog lovers.

However, I soon found out that someone higher agreed with Master Chief.

The three-star Admiral!

3.

AN EXTRAORDINARY ENLISTMENT

Big risks bring big success!

— ADMIRAL JOHN FISHER, in a
letter to Winston Churchill

The dog discussion died after we got to Japan. Life was busy; we had all the usual ship's work plus integrating into the forward-deployed Naval forces. We had to acclimate to a foreign country and to a different ocean and to a new base and to a new chain of command and to separation from our families and to new foods and to new customs—new everything except the ship. We even swapped thirty of our ship-mates for sailors with the frigate that was heading to the US after we relieved them of their duties.

The crew spent less time together when in port. We no longer had breakfast or dinner together to deliberate about mascots or other trivial pursuits, and lunch was less leisurely than those at sea. After we'd been in our new home port for a month, I decided that it was time for Phase II of the mascot *discussion*. I walked to the quarterdeck and had the Petty Officer of the Watch broadcast over the ship's speakers, "Ensign LaPointe, Ensign Johnston, report to the captain on the quarterdeck!"

Being summoned publicly by the captain is rare and raises alarm bells. Those two showed up breathless and wide-eyed, sporting matching "What have I done?" looks. Of course, I couldn't resist yanking their leashes a little more. I gave them a stern stare and motioned to follow me to my sedan. As we pulled away from the pier, I turned from the front seat. "Let's go to the animal shelter and *look* at what they have."

Storm clouds cleared and giant grins replaced furrowed brows.

We made the short drive to the other side of the naval base. There was no problem finding parking; in fact, there were no cars in sight. As we walked down the deserted road toward the shelter, I must have looked like a yakuza mob boss framed by two giant henchmen. My tactical orders: *Do not pick the first one you see. A suitable dog must weigh about twenty-five pounds, light enough to carry up and down the ship's ladders* (steep stairs) *yet big enough so it won't get stepped on.*

We were in a desolate area of the base, surrounded by a few timeworn industrial buildings that were long abandoned. It was so quiet that I could hear the birds singing and even the leaves of the few trees shivering in the light breeze. As we approached the shelter, we saw six canine detainees tethered outside. Five of them jumped up and barked, straining at their chains, raring to meet someone new. This shined a spotlight on the red dog lying in their midst, contemplating us with mild interest.

We petted them in turn. When I got to the redhead, I knelt and extended my hand. She delicately sniffed, triangle ears erect and focused forward, head slightly cocked as she studied me. She was beautiful despite her time in a kennel, a red fox with front paws elegantly crossed. Bemused dark eyes, with just a sliver of white around the edges of huge irises, appraised me. I wondered who was judging whom. She had a white crest extending from her chest down to her undercarriage— an inverse racing stripe that proved to be fitting—and the tips of her paws were trimmed in white. Her coat was medium length, smooth, reddish-golden with cinnamon highlights, and her bushy tail curled up toward her back when she stood up. Her feathers, the longer hair on her hind legs, were Creamsicle wisps of orangish-red and white, like those of a golden retriever.

She had it all: beauty, intelligence, and a quiet calm. What we didn't know was her independent personality, her strength of will, her street-honed adaptability, and her feminine ability to manipulate 225 men.

It was love at first sight. Our search was over!

We went inside to talk to the private first class about adoption. The Army, which ran veterinary clinics for all military services, is not known for flexibility with rules and regulations. There was immediate confusion: How can a ship adopt a dog? Nothing in their manual covered this situation. Being a commander in uniform, on a Navy base, moved things along. I signed the paperwork as Jenna's sponsor. She weighed twenty-eight pounds, and I could feel her ribs as I lifted her down from the aluminum table. The clinic estimated she was about two years old; we would never discover anything about her history. The breed listed on her record was "Sheba." We discovered later that she was a Shiba Inu...and quickly found out what *that* meant.

What was her story? How long had she been on the streets? Was she from a Navy family or from a Japanese home? Did someone let her loose because they had to transfer? Did she escape? She would prove that few things could detain her!

Although we never found out about her past, I visualized Jenna living a traditional life with a Japanese family until she got separated. I imagined her sitting in a tiny apartment listening to the sounds of the city. Japan is densely packed and everything—houses, cars, dogs—comes in economy-size packages. I imagined perhaps her owner took Jenna for short walks along the urban streets each morning before work and then for a stroll in one of the local parks after work. Jenna would see lots of people and a few dogs, with whom she'd exchange a formal sniff. Her owner would cook a small dinner for herself and serve Jenna's meal in a bright Hello Kitty bowl (which Jenna secretly hated...maybe that was why she left). They would settle in for some TV, catching one of those crazy game shows where contestants smile while getting the crap smacked out of them by a giant pink-padded battering ram. Jenna's life would have been pleasant, sedate, and orderly...everything around her pruned and clipped and clean. This, or an ordered life like it, was what I imagined Jenna had experienced before her induction into the US Navy.

Jenna was now assigned to the Navy's finest guided missile fast frigate. Her life had changed like that of no other dog, and our lives would change like that of no other Navy crew.

What was the first thing Jenna did on board? A grand ceremony to meet and greet the crew? A tour of her new quarters? No, I took her into the wardroom galley and bathed her with my shampoo in the deep sink where the dishes got washed. Probably broke a dozen sanitary regulations. She was rather fragrant, and we couldn't have a stinky sailor on board. She did *not* appreciate the bath, splaying her legs to stay out of the sink like one of those cartoon cats and then trying to leap out whenever she felt my hands relax.

My first taste of her iron will, and her first taste of mine. I established myself as the alpha male—at least that's what I thought.

Time would tell.

Matt and Nate went to the commissary (grocery store) to buy dog food, bowls, and other necessities that were not available through the Navy supply system. We were ill prepared. We planned for new crew arrivals many months in advance…yet this was what we called a "pop-up." A pop-up is an aircraft, missile, or ship that is detected at the last minute because it is at low altitude, small, or stealthy. Because it is close by the time we spy it, a pop-up requires immediate action.

Jenna had popped up in our lives, and we were now on her schedule.

Jenna met her new family—her shipmates—in many venues. In her first months she was skittish, unable to find her way around a "house" that was different than anything she had ever encountered. Than any dog had encountered. Instincts did not help, as her ancestors over nine centuries had never lived in an environment with no grass, trees, or other canines. She was disoriented on a metal ship smelling of oil, smoke, gunpowder, fried food, and men. Visitors to the ship often commented on the heavy oil/fuel/smoky scent, something we no longer noticed. A dog's sense of smell is ten thousand times more sensitive than ours…a common analogy is that humans can smell a teaspoon of sugar in their coffee, but Jenna could detect it in a million gallons of water. If ship smells were strong to humans, they must have been overpowering to her.

Add in 225 new friends who were anxious to meet her, many approaching too fast or too directly for her taste. The dog lovers took her on walks and rides and showed her around the ship. Jenna must have missed the peaceful shelter during her first days aboard, but she quickly found spots where she could have "me time."

Jenna was loved and cared for from day one. She soon discovered the "smoke deck," a small outside area amidships where sailors congregated to light a coffin nail and talk. Nonsmokers also hung out there to shoot the shit, and Jenna learned it was the place to see and be seen.

And more important, to collect off-the-record food handouts.

To my knowledge she never had a cigarette, but I am sure she tasted every foodstuff produced on the mess decks and every snack sold in the ship's store... despite my explicit orders that she not be fed anything but dog food.

Do you understand the fearsome power of a Navy Commanding Officer? Well, Jenna superseded this long-held law of the sea. And it wasn't even a close contest. Imagine her sitting at attention in front of you, foxy ears pointed at the sky, black mottled nose twitching in anticipation, licking her lips while glancing from your face to your hands and back again to meet your eyes.

Could *you* have resisted?

She gained ten pounds in her first month aboard, a 40 percent increase that filled out her frame.

Enlisting in the Navy is a decision that changes the path of one's life. Although Jenna's enlistment was more shanghaied than voluntary, she joined the *Vandy* crew and became famous throughout the fleet. I sensed that life on board had fundamentally changed but never imagined how adding one small red dog would alter the course of an American warship and her crew.

And the path of my career, and even of my life.

4.

FORTUNE FAVORS THE BOLD

*The difference between a good and great officer
is about ten seconds.*

— ADMIRAL ARLEIGH BURKE, World War II Hero

The Navy is serious business, the ledger measured not in dollars but in lives. General Alexander A. Vandegrift was a hero who turned the tide of World War II at Guadalcanal, then went on to save the Marine Corps during postwar budget cuts. For these actions he was awarded the Medal of Honor and had a ship named after him.

Our ship.

The Battle of Guadalcanal was the first step of the US island-hopping campaign, a bloody path that led to victory over Japan. We paid a high price for the freedom we enjoy today. More than twenty-six thousand Marines and soldiers died during the battle for Guadalcanal, and thousands of sailors died in the associated sea battles. That's thirty thousand fathers, sons, and uncles...equal to the population of many small towns. The general was a war hero, beating the Japanese for the first time on one of their reinforced islands. Many thought it could not be done, but he found a way. He landed his Marines and dug in for a fight against an enemy prepared to die to the last man. He was bold and innovative, aggressive and tenacious.

He led from the front. He won.

That was our legacy, that was how we prepared to fight. We had to channel General Vandegrift's brilliant leadership, tactical acumen, and toughness to win the next battle in a digital world that moved at Mach 7.

The Navy exists to fight battles at sea. It was difficult to keep that mission, which was improbable, at the forefront of our minds. There were many everyday items demanding our time and attention. Training to fight the ship against a formidable enemy sometimes seemed to be nothing more than an academic drill. It was easy to lose focus on the "main thing" when submerged by inspections, personnel issues, administrative requirements, and daily living.

But we made ourselves train like we expected to fight. Why?

Think of it this way. You are going to duel with another person, and one or both of you will be shot. Try to imagine yourself in that position. Ponder the life-changing, even life-ending, results from just one minute of your life. How much time and effort would you put into preparing?

Fortune favors the bold...but advance preparations improve your chances.

Our lives would be on the line, so preparations for the conflict took precedence over all else. This is how the best ships view maintenance and training, as logical steps to optimize their chance of surviving—and triumphing—in battle.

We also possessed a secret weapon: a bold redhead with a rakish grin. Although Jenna did not have prescribed battle duties, she did have a station in the combat information center (CIC) where we directed the fight. Each sailor reached down and raked her back as she sauntered past, like dipping fingers in a warm current as you float downriver. Jenna did not alter course or speed, but she left a trail of grinning shipmates in her wake. As the crew dressed out in battle gear to protect themselves from fire and shrapnel, the junior sailor "helped" Jenna don her gear. Jenna knew this scenario, scampering away when she saw the heavy Nomex hood that protected the crew from flash burns. It took two seamen to catch her and pull the hood on as she squirmed and tossed her head from side to side. After a struggle, Jenna sat, sad brown eyes peeking out from the tan hoodie. Although these hoods got washed...once in a while...the sweaty residue of many previous wearers assaulted her keen nose.

As soon as everyone became engaged in their combat jobs, she pulled the hood off with her front paws.

And then hid it.

The CIC was kept darkened so we could see the tactical displays, so there were many corners and spots that were infrequently visited. We often found flash hoods stashed behind status boards when we turned on the lights once in port.

War at sea is not glamorous. We are unlikely to ever see our opponent, except as a blip on radar or sonar. We might not even know if our ship is being targeted. Most of the crew work deep within the ship, mole-like senses on edge, waiting for a cave-in. At any moment a disastrous strike may shatter the ship, bringing flames, deadly smoke, icy water, or instant death. Sailors cannot evacuate to avoid a fire because *we* are the fire department. We can't just run outside to escape. We have a macabre saying that *the flooding will eventually put out the fires*.

There have been two significant attacks on Oliver Hazard Perry-class frigates, the same ship type as *Vandegrift*. The USS *Stark* (FFG-31) was hit by two Iraqi Exocet missiles in 1987 during the Iran-Iraq War. Although one missile failed to explode, the damage to the ship was extensive and thirty-one sailors died. The crew fought fires and flooding throughout the night, enabling the ship to make it back to port. Eight months later, the USS *Samuel B. Roberts* (FFG-58) struck an Iranian mine, blasting a fifteen-foot hole in the side and breaking her keel. Normally when this "backbone" is severed, the ship goes down. In this case, the crew battled flooding to save the ship. Ten sailors were critically wounded.

Navy ships are compartmentalized, which means they have watertight doors and hatches to isolate parts of the ship in order to contain flooding or fires. As Jenna traversed the ship, she had to jump a watertight doorframe every ten to fifteen feet. She trotted up to these "knee-knockers," gathered herself like a horse going over a barrier, then jumped over the foot-high doorframe. She grew accustomed to this odd agility test and moved around the ship easily, even when it was rolling with the waves.

Watertight doors confined fire and flooding, but the huge engineering spaces below the waterline contained generators and other critical equipment. We couldn't just close some doors and let them flood or burn. The crew would have to climb down ladders into the fire and water—blinded by black smoke—trusting their shipmates to keep them alive as they battled for the ship's life. Those ladders, which serve as stairs on a ship, are as steep as the ladder that you would lean against your house. A slip could end in pin-balling one's head against hard, inanimate objects during a ten-foot fall, then breaking that fall, and said head, on an unyielding metal deck. This was not a hypothetical risk: an officer on board fell down a ladder and broke his back. We took care when climbing those steel ladders, especially when the ship was bucking in high seas.

Jenna climbed the ship's ladders; she scaled those tall vertical steps with rails that connected different levels of the ship. She would stop at the bottom of a ladder, judge the height and ship's roll, and then *walk* up the ladder during the few seconds of calm between waves. Most human visitors were afraid to climb the ladders while stationary in port, and they had fingers and opposable thumbs! Jenna never fell because she knew her limits. Coming down a ladder was much more difficult, since she could not hold onto the rails, and a dog's depth perception is not as good as ours. She would not attempt to come down but instead waited at the top of the ladder for a human elevator.

You may be envisaging a red dog sitting patiently for the next sailor to come by...but that was not the case. When Jenna was ready to move, she was ready *now*. She would stand at the top, looking down to see if someone was coming up, then turn around to see if someone was going down. She never barked but quickly got her point across. I can still picture her staring at me from above, willing me to climb the ladder and carry her down. Which I did, as did everyone else. You've waited far longer for an elevator than Jenna ever waited for a sailor-vator.

We ordinarily went down ladders like you walk down stairs, back to the ladder and lightly gripping the handrails in case we lost footing on the steep steps.

That method is a little risky, but faster. If waves were throwing us around or the steps were slippery, we went down the ladder like you do at home, facing the ladder and backing down. And that was how we went down with Jenna. We picked her up with both arms—she was a solid thirty pounds from frequent snacks—and then tucked her under our right armpit, right arm and hand under her breastbone, like a football that we didn't want to fumble. Then we backed up to the ladder, grabbed the left handrail with our left hand, and slowly climbed down. Jenna was unusually compliant and stayed still for the descent, seemingly aware of the danger. When the weather was bad, the descent was more harrowing.

Fortune favors the bold. We worked hard to keep focused on our deadly mission, but constant training eventually grows cold and mundane without relief. We did some things on *Vandy* that, had they gone wrong, would have gone badly for me. As in fired. I took measured risks to build confidence and morale...keys to winning at sea. Many captains viewed coming alongside an oiler at twenty-five knots as a cowboy approach, too much risk of miscue. I took that risk to minimize our time alongside the oiler and thereby reduce our tactical vulnerability in a hostile environment. The safer formula was to toe the line, keep behavior beyond reproach, don't wander outside of the norms, and get promoted—safe, but not how we grow the next Nimitz or Vandegrift. I would be forced to take extraordinary risks when we visited Hong Kong.

Of course, enlisting an abandoned dog against the norms of a regulated society was rather *bold*. Animal mascots were common during World War II, assuaging the stabbing stress of combat by providing companionship between battles or during tedious months at sea. Naval dogs went ashore with the crew to find food and provide early warning of danger. The Marine Corps still maintains "Chesty," a bulldog mascot named after hero Lewis B. "Chesty" Puller. Unfortunately, mammal mascots were replaced on board ships in the 1950s by smaller creatures such as fish and lizards. Jenna's enlistment on *Vandy* was just restoring a once-favored tradition that provided comfort to sailors far from home. After all, it's not gratifying to pet a fish or hug a reptile.

5.

WHERE DOES JENNA *GO?*

There's this misconception that
the Navy is this cruise ship
and you get to go out and sail around,
and every now and then,
you have to swab the deck.
But, no, it is a very impressive group
of young people that live at sea,
in this place that's very uncomfortable.
They exude a pride that is well-deserved.

— TOM HANKS

"I love the fuckin' Navy, and the Navy loves fuckin'
me!" This fleet refrain captures both our elemen-
tal love of the Navy, as well as our recognition
that the Navy is a titanic bureaucracy that could run us
over without even realizing we were there. Yet we are all
volunteers, and many make a career of it. It *is* a tough
life: difficult work in rough conditions, long separations
from family, low pay, and few benefits. However, the
Navy is also a calling. Not perhaps the sweet beckoning

songs of the Sirens, but more that chafing tune you can't get out of your head. In this case, that irritating tune might be "In the Navy."

First and foremost, sailors are patriotic and understand that their sacrifice makes a difference—a difference to the United States and a difference to the entire world. Their efforts improve the likelihood of enduring peace or, if that fails, ensure that we can beat up whoever has broken that peace. We like being part of a team, especially a winning team. This esprit de corps and teamwork, aimed at a loftier goal than profitability, cannot be matched in the civilian sector. More on that later.

Sailors are not just patriots but also the ultimate survivors. They volunteer to live for four to six years on a ship where they don't know anyone. Compare this to the participants on *Survivor*, who strive to last thirty-nine days on a beach somewhere in the tropics. They grow thin, tired, cold, and cranky. Often the veneer of civilized behavior wears off to reveal a baser side. At the end there is a celebration for the person who "survived" this ordeal. Contrast that with enlisting in the Navy.

A young eighteen-year-old decides he wants to build a better life, to see the world, or to find a career. Often, he accomplishes all three. He joins the Navy with little or no knowledge of what is ahead, putting his life into someone else's hands for the next six years. His rainbow is not a million dollars or becoming famous on TV, but rather to serve his country and to better himself. His beach will be gray and hard, covered in non-skid, at times so hot that the soles of his shoes will melt. He will often spend more than thirty-nine days at sea—I was once at sea for 122 continuous days—and deploy away from home and family for six to nine months at a time. He may not have to find his own food, but he will have little time to enjoy it in a mess (cafeteria) deep within the ship. He won't have to find water, though it may sometimes smell of fuel, and he may have to go without showers. He won't need fire or shelter; sailors sleep in large shared berthing areas with bunks squeezed in three-high. He will not be lounging on a mat waiting for the day to end but will be working hard for many hours, night and day.

A sailor will visit foreign ports, but that will comprise about 1 percent of his time on a ship. He will suffer enduring stress, long and tedious hours, and in the end may not be allowed to stay in the Navy. There is no hidden immunity idol to keep his torch lit. He will not become famous or rich, and his journey will take much longer than thirty-nine days...and be far more arduous. He may face real danger, work in perilous conditions, have days or months when it is work-eat-sleep-repeat without end, live in a rolling-pitching-smelly tin can with some people he hates, with no power to change anything, helpless to escape a bad day. He cannot opt out...he *must* survive.

What is life like on a Navy ship? It is just like home, except for a few *woulds* and *wouldn'ts*. You *would* go for six months without seeing your family. You *wouldn't* relax every day "after work," change into comfortable clothes, and put your feet up on the couch to catch your favorite show. You *wouldn't* need to worry about driving, though you *would* have family automobile issues thousands of miles away. You *would* need to reset the alarm clock each night based upon your rotating watch schedule. You *would* watch an internal channel showing a dated movie or the Armed Forces Channel that *would* periodically be pixelated and never show anything you would normally have watched. You *would* get to participate in drills simulating fire, flooding, or nuclear attack wearing gear that is heavy, hot, and stinks of the last twelve guys who sweated in it. You *would* share your "bedroom" with eighty-one neighbors who have varied work and watch schedules, and whose alarms *would* be sounding off at all hours. You *would* eat with those same neighbors in a cafeteria where you shove food into your mouth with one hand while using the other to stop your plate from sliding across the table due to the swell.

On *Vandy*, you *would* bend to pet Jenna as she waited for someone's plate to slide off the table. Jenna brought a little bit of home to our steel house. She asked no questions, demanded no answers, and did not distinguish based on rank. She also became a star attraction when the younger sailors figured out that she was a chick magnet. Jenna's cuteness was a big part of that attraction, but a dog also created a risk-free environment for girls to approach while cooing indecipherable words.

Jenna was a *chick electromagnet*, and *Vandy*'s single sailors quickly deciphered her charismatic code. What girl could pass up a sailor sporting his best uniform and parading a foxy red dog? Both sailor and Jenna ramrod-straight from toes to neck, heads high, happiness stretching along the blue leash as they sought a grassy area among the piers and buildings. Their trail often took them through the Navy Exchange (NEX) area. The NEX is the Navy's Walmart, selling everything from clothes to furniture. Located in a small mall with the commissary, food court, laundromat, travel office, and barbershop, it is the hub of base activity. *Vandy* sailors figured out that the most strategic location to see and be seen was the bench area between the parking lot and the mall.

Jenna spent many hours sitting beside a bench putting up with admirers new and old, an unwilling center of attention. She took on a new level of popularity among her shipmates, becoming the hottest fishing lure as tales of her magnetic appeal spread. The single guys now vied with the dog lovers for a chance to walk her. Jenna started getting *too many* walks. Eventually quarterdeck watch standers had to keep track of her treks to ensure she was not walked to exhaustion.

A Navy ship is immaculate. Even one with a dog.

Let me reiterate. A ship full of men, without women to oversee them, was always ultraclean. Sounds unlikely, even to me!

At 0600 (6:00 a.m.) the boatswain's mate of the watch would broadcast, "Reveille, reveille. All hands heave out and trice up!" over speakers throughout the ship. Translation: get your ass out of the rack (bed) and fasten it (the rack, that is) in the stowed position. Almost immediately another loud and annoying bosun's piping and, "Sweepers, sweepers, man your brooms. Make a clean sweep down fore and aft. Sweep down all decks, ladders, and passageways."

Why were we so keen to keep the ship sparkling, when men are renowned procrastinators when it comes to cleaning? As always, part of it was tradition. Ships of yore sailed for many months with rotting food on board, hoping to catch some rain for water. Sailors were packed into small spaces, so anything contagious ran rampant. Disease was frequent and deadly. Sailors learned through the ages that they must keep their ship clean or die, and thus the origin of the term "shipshape."

Have you ever heard of a modern Navy ship having a contagious disease ramble through it like happens on cruise ships? In today's 24/7 news environment, it would be a headline for days. We kept the berthing so cold that sometimes you could see your breath...and any germs in that breath quickly died.

The cleanliness of a ship reflects pride of ownership and professionalism, projecting a trim, warfighting appearance. Our message to friends and enemies alike is, *We're ready to do battle, and we even have time to polish the brass daily!* We washed the ship frequently to get the salt off and conducted a freshwater wash-down before entering port. We loved a good rainstorm—we'd chase a storm spotted on the radar to get a good wash. For special occasions we'd even paint while at sea, putting guys over the side to touch up the haze-gray hull.

The XO spent an hour every day inspecting berthing areas and facilities. This was affectionately known as "heads [toilets] and beds." He inspected every area with a select team, then directed corrective measures. We held quarterly zone inspections where all the officers and chiefs spent half a day scrutinizing every space for safety hazards, damage control issues, and cleanliness. *Every* space. Notes were taken, compiled, and required actions tracked. We missed nothing!

As usual, Jenna was the outlier. The most frequent questions about Jenna were, "Where does she go to the bathroom?" and, "Who has to clean it up?" The standard answer to part one was, *wherever she wants*. But Jenna was fastidious, a trait of her breed, and judicious about where she left her mark. There was no grass or sandbox on the ship. She learned to do her business on the decks outside the skin of the ship. A ship is divided up so that sailors are responsible for the areas in which they work. This is true outside as well, so there were invisible lines marking the territories of the different tribes on board, lines that not even Jenna could detect. Where she decided to squat determined who cleaned up. Inside was also divvied up between the different divisions, but the JORG ensign was responsible for all indoor "Jenna spills." This fell to Matt "Be Careful What You Ask For" LaPointe, who handled these accidents until he got promoted and passed the duty on.

Jenna was confused during her first days aboard. The Shiba Inu is an ancient breed, but even her long lineage did not provide clues for how to live on a ship. On her maiden voyage, Jenna was still getting accustomed to the ship and not appreciating being rocked about. Just after 8:00 p.m. the boatswain's mate piped a call to attention over the loudspeaker, and after an elongated pause—a suppressed giggle was audible—he announced with glee coloring every word, "Away the Poopie Team, away the Poopie Team. Jenna spill in radio P-way."

The crew exploded in laughter. When I opened my cabin door, I was assailed by shouts of glee rising from the main deck. Matt trudged to radio, where he found a mess.

And a growing number of amused shipmates.

How could one small dog, even reacting to her new and unusual circumstances, put out that much poop and pee? To make matters worse, when the ship heeled, the urine spread to every corner of this long passageway. Matt had trouble containing the spill, as areas already cleaned got "reinvigorated" by yellow waves.

Ship corridors are called passageways, "P-ways" for short. We now had a more amusing reason to call them "Pee-ways." Unfortunately for Matt and the line of JORGs after him, Jenna had spills from time to time. The inevitable loudspeaker calls to action were always met with unanimous—with the exception of one ensign—elation. Hard to believe dog urine could do so much for crew morale, something not addressed in the commanding officer's manual.

The JORG ensign figured out it was in his best interest to take Jenna outside a few times daily to prevent having to swab up internal spills. One day he could not get Jenna to do her business, despite his best efforts. JORG had a watch coming up and did not have time to wait while she nosed around. By then we understood that Jenna did what *she* wanted, not what *we* wanted. He was carrying her back down the ladder when he may have squeezed a little too hard...and received a warm golden shower as a result.

You know what happened next.

"Away the Poopie Team, away...!"

6.

RED NUNNS WITH GREEN CANS

He that will not sail till all dangers are over
must never put to sea.

— THOMAS FULLER, English churchman and historian

I clung to the railing as I watched the 592-foot USS *Willamette* ram the 529-foot USS *Jason*. A lieutenant at the time, I had been summoned to *Jason*'s bridge just in time to witness the calamity. *Willamette* sliced through our hull, and sailors stumbled across that ship's forecastle (bow) to exit their space, unaware of where they were or what was happening in the fire, smoke, and confusion. *Willamette*—sailors soon nicknamed her *We'll Ram It*—reversed engines to pull out of the forty-foot gaping hole. The ocean was on fire, burning oil from punctured tanks forming blazing pools that lit the surreal scene. Thirty-five years later I can still smell the smoke and feel the numb helplessness as I gazed, immobilized, upon this catastrophe.

One chief died and eight sailors were seriously injured.

We fought fires for two days, drifting at sea, before getting them under control. Because we were uncertain if the ship would remain intact—*Jason* was nearly cut in half despite her heavy steel plating—we had to be towed backward...slowly...to Pearl Harbor.

How can ships run into one another when the ocean is enormous and there is so little traffic? Collisions between ships are rare, but when one does occur it is noteworthy because of the size and value of the vessels. Driving a ship is much more complicated than driving a car. There are no roads, no handy lines delineating where the ship should be driving, no speed limit markers...or cement medians...or police to enforce safe driving. There are no stoplights at sea, so mariners treat each ship meeting like entering an invisible roundabout. A ship rides on a moving carpet of water rather than a fixed hardtop road. When you steer your car, either going forward or backward, it goes in that direction. Your car has brakes that will stop your momentum within a few car lengths. Brakes are a car's best advantage; if in doubt, you just slow or stop until you figure it out. On our ship, we had to reverse the rotation of the propellers. It took thousands of yards to stop a warship, miles to stop merchant vessels. If we slowed the ship, it lost steerageway, the ability to steer. If you turn your car quickly, your tires immediately respond to the wheel. A warship's turning radius to complete a U-turn is five hundred to eight hundred yards, and more than double that for merchants.

Just like there are rules for driving your car, there are "rules of the road" designed to prevent collisions at sea. These rules cover all aspects of safe navigation on the high seas: steering and sailing rules, lights and shapes displayed, sound and light signals. Following the rules of the road is essential to safe navigation, for without them it would be a total *goat rope*—Navy slang for when something seemingly simple, like roping a goat, becomes a disaster. Despite the complications of driving watercraft, most anyone can take out a small boat. It is all too common for small boats to approach a ship closely, too closely, to get a picture or to wave to us.

The mnemonic "Even Red Nunns Have Odd Green Cans" reminds sailors that even-numbered red buoys with a conical "nun's cap" are to starboard (right) when entering a harbor, while odd-numbered green can-shaped buoys are to port (left). At least that is true in the US, but it would lead us up the wrong side of the channel in China...a scenario we would face in Shanghai.

The cost of a collision like *Jason*'s is high—in lives, in dollars, and in loss of warfighting readiness. In 2016–17 the Navy suffered an unprecedented chain of collisions and groundings that led to a complete overhaul of training and certification requirements. The ship's Officer of the Deck (OOD) is responsible for safe navigation. The Commanding Officer places his full trust and confidence in this officer to make smart decisions. One of my sharpest, and also most dodgy, OODs was Lieutenant J. R. Reyes. Of Filipino descent, J. R. was five feet five inches tall, more round than not, cherubic face always on the verge of a wide grin. He reported aboard *Vandy* just before we sailed to Japan. He made a dramatic entrance at the last moment, leaving him hours for a turnover of duties that should have taken days. We learned there was drama on his side as well. When he first got to the pier, the ship was gone and the gate guard mistakenly informed him that we had deployed overseas. J. R. thought he had missed ship's movement, a quick end to a short career. Lucky for him the ship was just out for one day.

We had few "windows" on *Vandy*, only two small portholes. We first spied J. R. from the porthole in the wardroom as he rushed down the pier dragging his suitcase. The other porthole was in my cabin, looking out to starboard. J. R. confessed, many years later, that when he was driving the ship and was going to pass close to another ship that he had not reported to me—as required—he made sure it passed down our port side.

My blind side.

Jenna decided that she liked J. R.'s rack. It was near the wardroom (food), not too high off the ground, and had a curtain that was usually drawn to keep it dark. She hot racked there when J. R. was working, eating, or on watch. Hot racking is when two sailors share one rack due to overcrowding; the rack is occupied night and day, keeping it hot.

J. R. was not a natural dog lover, so we assumed that Jenna would have to find new digs. But his relaxed manner extended to her, even when he returned to his stateroom exhausted from a long watch. He would pull back his rack curtain to find a curled red ball on his pillow and slide her over so he could scoot in. Jenna, not a natural people-lover, usually decided it was time to find a new spot and would jump down from his rack. The officers enjoyed this power struggle for dozing dominance, but eventually Jenna and J. R. worked out their routines so that it became the status quo. They maintained this cordial détente, each claiming co-ownership of one treasured den. Each willing to let sleeping dogs—and humans—lie.

Even Red Dogs have Odd Rack Partners!

7.

JENNA BANNED!

*Nelson's greatest achievements
were all solely due to his disobeying orders!
Any fool can obey orders!*

— FLEET ADMIRAL JOHN FISHER

Six loud gongs reverberated throughout the ship, announcing the arrival of the 3-star Fleet Commander. I was standing on the quarterdeck with the XO, Master Chief, and Officer of the Deck, all of us in newly pressed khaki uniforms, shined shoes, and trimmed hair with squared sideburns extending from beneath our red ball caps. His sedan stopped and the driver jumped out and hastily opened the rear door. Vice Admiral Nathaniel Blacker[1] slowly emerged and stood scanning the ship, oblivious to the welcoming committee standing at attention a few yards away. He was the supreme kingpin, with the power to do whatever he wanted. I watched for any reaction, wondering if his first impression of the ship was as positive as mine had been a few months ago. His lips remained pursed, eyebrows straight across, a professional poker player unwilling to tip his hand.

The Admiral was tall, over six feet, his coifed raven-black hair shining and radiant against his pale skin. He was a fighter pilot whose call sign was "Slacker," though as someone many levels below him I certainly wouldn't be calling him by that informal moniker. Aviators' call signs are branded on them early in their career, usually related to their surname, some blunder, or a personal trait worthy of ridicule. In this case the Admiral's surname was the baseline for his call sign—I was quite certain he had never slacked in his life. Just the opposite—he had rocketed up through the ranks, making a name for himself in the halls of the Pentagon. Rumor had it that he would soon wear four stars.

The Admiral crossed the brow (gangway) at the slow pace that belongs to royalty and the homeless. We stood at rigid attention on the quarterdeck, saluting him as he stepped on board. I shook his hand, returning his firm grip while looking him in the eye. He held my gaze, unblinking, for a few long seconds while maintaining a brilliant smile. He looked more like a movie star than someone in the Navy. We pride ourselves on looking neat and squared away, but he had taken it a few octaves higher with his dyed hair and whitened teeth.

I introduced him to my leaders and the watch standers. He was gracious, asking innocuous questions to further engage the younger petty officers. He turned, ready to go, and I led him through the ship to my cabin. He was silent along the route, without the normal questions or comments. The only "cabin" on this ship belonged to me. It was located high and forward in the ship so I could reach the bridge quickly while at sea. About ten by ten feet, my cabin contained a small head, a pull-down narrow rack, a desk, and two small couches welded to the deck.

I seated the Admiral at the nearest couch and sat facing him on the other. I surreptitiously removed a wisp of red hair—there were always a few remnants of Jenna on her favorite at-sea bed regardless of how often it was cleaned. Jenna was sheltering in place many decks below us, no doubt napping in a stateroom. I wanted to avoid any possibility of drama during the Admiral's first call on us.

I offered coffee; he waved his hand to decline. The smile was gone. I wondered if he had spotted something that concerned him on his short trip up here. I took another quick glance. His dark eyes regarded me from his hawkish face, assessing me. He was only here for a brief visit, so I was anxious to get him to the flight deck to address the crew. Expecting pleasantries, I was unprepared for his two-pronged attack.

Holding my gaze, he questioned why the crew was wearing red ball caps rather than the prescribed blue. OK, that was unexpected but a softball pitch I could handle. I explained that we had a special dispensation from the Secretary of the Navy allowing us to wear red ball caps with gold stitching (the proud colors of the US Marine Corps) in honor of General Vandegrift. I didn't bother to explain what he already knew—that the general won the Battle of Guadalcanal and became the Commandant of the Marine Corps, where he saved that proud branch from being disestablished.

The Admiral fixed me with raptor eyes, his beakish nose aimed at me, and asked how old the letter was. I searched his face for some sign that he was putting me on but saw no humor in his obsidian eyes. I offered to show him the letter, which had been written about ten years earlier. He waved his arm dismissively, stating that a paper signed by a secretary three times removed was worthless. This was no place for me to argue, to point out that these dispensations were good until cancelled, to highlight the esprit de corps benefits of our red ball caps.

This was not turning out to be the anticipated get-to-know-you coffee.

We couldn't have pissed him off with our perfor-mance, because we had outperformed our sister ships on his waterfront. I was in a bit of shock, my mind reel-ing as I considered the ramifications to the crew. I was suddenly eager for him return to the flagship to concen-trate on bigger things than my ship.

But the Admiral did not make a move to leave. My heart, normally calm in any situation, started to beat faster.

What now?

Would he order the ship to cut circles in the frigid waters off Korea for endless days? He had that kind of power.

"I hear you have a dog on board."

He leaned into me, eyes cold and smile predatory. He sensed a weak spot and was enjoying batting the mouse around. I nodded, my throat tightening, tensing for the hammer blow. It came quickly.

"Well, I don't think *that* is a good idea either."

He stood; conversation complete.

I stood at attention, waiting for a normalizing handshake that never came. I opened the door and led him to the flight deck, where the crew was assembled. It was a blur of faces as we went down ladders and through passageways, my mind whirling with implications and consequences.

No red ball caps, a proud *Vandy* tradition for more than a decade?

No Jenna?!

I needed time to think this through, something I should have done before adopting a stray dog on a Navy combatant. She had only been on board for a couple of months but had already become part of the crew and a comfort to sailors separated from their families. Jenna was a little piece of home that we treasured when we went to sea. These changes would be a double-barreled blast to my sailors' red-and-gold hearts.

As we arrived at the flight deck, I wondered what the Admiral would tell the crew, what he had in store for them. Would he announce his staggering intentions, or was he saving something even more horrific?

The Master Chief handed the microphone to the Admiral, professional as always and looking squared away in his khaki uniform and red ball cap. I looked out at the silent formation: a sea of blue uniforms topped with *red ball caps*.

Oh jeez, he is going to slaughter us.

The Admiral took the microphone, favoring Mike with an affable grin, and turned toward the two hundred sailors eager to hear from him. Something was different. His posture was easy and relaxed as he looked out at those young faces. "How ya'll doin'?" he drawled. "Welcome to the forward-deployed naval forces!" He drifted toward the formation, comfortable on stage. "Sorry I haven't been over sooner, but I am happy to see ya'll and have heard nuthin' but wunderful thangs about this here ship. Please stand easy, relax. I just want to say a few words and then I will answer any questions ya'll have."

The crew was entranced and enchanted by this homey Admiral standing among them. I looked down and shook my head.

My mind was racing as I saluted the Admiral while the Officer of the Deck rendered honors for his departure. I was confused, uncertain of what would come next. Jenna and our red ball caps set the crew apart from the crowd, making us special.

I held an emergency triad meeting that evening. The XO and CMC came up with a plan to wear blue ball caps when in port and red ball caps only while at sea. It was middle ground that would temporarily keep the ship out of the crosshairs.

As to Jenna's disfavor, I kept this troubling item to myself, for once not sharing with my most trusted advisers. Although the Admiral's words could have been construed as an order—and I was built to carry out orders—I could also make the case that he had only suggested her removal. This response felt wrong, a sea lawyer's quibbling to avoid an unwelcome order from a senior officer. A *very senior* officer.

Waffling because I didn't like the decision.

I had a tough decision to make that would impact crew morale, the ship's reputation...and my career. Without the XO and Master Chief's advice. Normally quick to make decisions, my mind was shrouded in dense fog.

The next day I sat at my desk immersed in thought, the sounds of everyday ship life providing a comforting concerto. The deep hum of a generator being tested could be felt as much as heard, the squeaking of the ladder as someone climbed to the bridge, the metallic squelch as a watertight door was closed and tightened. A cold nose nudged me from my reverie, pushing against my hand. I looked down into Jenna's unblinking dark eyes as she watched me intently, sitting ramrod straight next to my chair. I scratched her head and then under her chin as she continued to look at me, for once accepting human attention.

"That's OK, girl, we won't send you back to the pound."

Jenna stood and strolled over to the couch. She hopped up, twirled around once, then laid down in a nose-to-tail ball. Her gaze continued to hold mine.

She huffed and closed her eyes.

8.

LIBERTY HOUND

Not all who wander are lost.

— J. R. R. TOLKIEN

Jenna was an escape artist, the prototypical Navy *liberty hound*. A liberty hound is a sailor who takes full advantage of every port visit, the first to depart the ship when it arrives and the last to return aboard. Jenna was certainly in that club. She had only two modes: lying down or moving en route to some objective, with little time for senseless wandering or impractical visiting. On board I observed her trotting along passageways daily, stopping to investigate something new or interesting. Jenna was her own dog and not constrained by the regulations that bound the rest of us. She did not know, or care, about being UA (Unauthorized Absence) or AWOL (Absent WithOut Leave) when she left the ship. She wasn't running away; she just felt the need to go on liberty—by herself—from time to time.

The three watch standers on the quarterdeck stood between her and freedom, and they knew the narrow brow was her only path off the ship. When they spotted her trotting toward the brow, they would rush to block her way. Shifty and fast, she was untouchable, hitting the hole like an NFL running back, accelerating down the brow, ears back and impervious to shouted commands. Her hundred-yard sprint down the pier would have shattered any Olympic record. Jenna slowed when she got to the road, knowing she was free to roam. Despite searching for and then chasing her many times, I never detected a pattern to her wanderings. Was she seeking other dogs? Food? It seemed she was just seeking freedom from the ship's confines...until dinner was served.

The base police became very familiar with Jenna. They called us when they saw her, but after several attempts didn't even try to apprehend the dog they nicknamed the "Red Rocket." They even kept the ship's phone number on speed dial so they could quickly give us location data. The *Vandy* crew would then organize a search party that employed Navy Search and Rescue tactics to locate Jenna. We initiated a sector search, which was like cutting up a pie; starting at her last known position, each person walked outward looking in a sector. This was a proven Navy search pattern used in wide swaths of ocean. But Jenna did not drift serenely with the current, nor did she cooperate when spotted. She often made it back to the ship before our search parties did. Since we had no way to recall the searchers, sailors straggled back over the next hour to find her sleeping on the quarterdeck.

The base police went out of their way to inform the ship of Jenna's location so that she would not get hurt or lost. They were clearly looking out for the Rocket. Luckily, no reports on Jenna made it to Admiral Blacker, which would have ended her time on the ship. And quite possibly mine.

Jenna had probably ended up in the pet shelter after running onto the Navy base from town and then being unable to find her way off the base. Fortunately, she never wandered outside the gates of the base, which would have ended her luck. Our advantage on the naval base was that there were walls and gates, and far fewer people and cars than in town. Although she could get under one of the gates, that gate was far from the ship. Her time as a stray had made her street smart, so she made it safely across innumerable streets on her way to greener pastures.

Jenna loved to run, but eventually her fun meter was pegged and it would be time to find a place for dinner. Even rockets run out of fuel. If she did not make it back to the ship for dinner, she visited either my house or that of Ensign Slim Pickens, one of my officers. We both lived in housing on base and had dogs that Jenna liked to play with. I would hear Sake barking in my small fenced backyard, and there would be Jenna with her nose stuck between the chain links exchanging pleasantries. I would open the gate and she would rush in, eager for some play-fighting with my larger dog. They were soon lapping water between pants and looking for bowls of food.

Jenna's most infamous—and dangerous—breakout occurred during a port call in Karachi, Pakistan. This port, which lies in the Indian Ocean close to the Arabian Gulf, was one of the few available in that region for ships to visit. Destitute and dangerous, this Islamic country forbade alcohol and had few attractions—it was on sailors' "Bottom 10" list of places to spend their precious liberty. Armed conflict was never far away, and organized crime ran a massive drug trade. Poverty, drugs, conflict with India and Afghanistan...Karachi simmered in desperation. Osama bin Laden would be found in this country that was still cloaked in extreme fundamentalism, hidden for years from the most intense global manhunt ever conducted.

Vandy was *awarded* a port call in Karachi and arrived without enthusiasm. Dead animals floating in the harbor near the ship added ambiance to the steaming cauldron of sewage, pollution, and rot that permeated the air. The buildings were stained brown, the air tepid and sepia-toned. Although the attack on USS *Cole* in Yemen was several months in the future, the *Vandy* stationed sentries armed with rifles based on the palpable threat. Pakistani marine sentries guarded the pier, menacing black machine guns hanging from their shoulders in a ready position as they stood facing us. They were locked and loaded.

Were they guarding the ship or guarding against the ship?

These young guards showed none of the normal exuberance of twenty-year-olds but stood tight-lipped and expressionless. There was little doubt that they would shoot first, then ask questions. The State Department officially warned the *Vandy* that it was forbidden to take firearms off the ship *under any circumstances*. They wanted to avoid an international incident at all costs.

Senior Chief Tony Fortson was the Officer of the Deck on the quarterdeck as the ship moored. He was attempting to keep his starched white uniform clean in the fetid environment and prevent his holstered sidearm from smudging his trousers. He had to coordinate dozens of details to get the ship hooked up to the pier and also deal with local vendors and keep the ship secure from any threat. Jenna's presence was lost in the confusion of the milling crowd, and as the brow came down, the Red Rocket seized the opportunity to zip off.

So what if no one else was excited about going on liberty. She was!

Tony knew that if she reached the end of the pier and went into the chaotic city, it would be her last trip. He had seconds to react, to decide what to do among all the activity surrounding him. He sprinted across the brow and jumped onto the pier, legs pumping and heart racing. Fortunately, Jenna was not moving at her normal sprint. Confused by all the movement around her and assaulted by bizarre smells, she was walking toward the gate. Tony, a six-foot-four giant topped by a crew cut, was a moving blur of white.

Too late, he realized that he had a handgun holstered on his hip.

He glanced ahead at the pier guards, who were watching this drama unfold, machine guns raised halfway to level.

Jenna or International Incident?

Tony did not break stride. With the sounds of harbor machinery masking his approach, he scooped Jenna up before she sensed his presence...just yards from the end of the pier and the armed sentinels.

Yards from entering the simmering city.

Yards from a death sentence.

Tony turned and walked back to the ship as nonchalantly as possible with his squirming package.

The liberty hound was confined to quarters after the quickest liberty call in history.

9.

DA KINE DOG

#1 Killing Platform: USS Vandegrift

— Admiral Yoshihiro Sakaue (Aug. 1, 1998)

The wail of a lone bagpipe filled the ship, calling the crew to battle. Long, slow notes drifted across the water, bouncing off the tropical seas. Those without a drop of Scottish or Irish blood still felt the ancient lust for combat, hearts and breaths quickening, eyes and minds sharpened...even if this was just an exercise. Lieutenant (Junior Grade) Dan Vasser stood on the bridge wing in plaid regalia, ruddy cheeks expanding to pipe a traditional Irish ballad. We were fighting a simulated war in RIMPAC 98 (Rim of the Pacific 1998), the largest naval exercise in the world. An exercise is a training event where ships and aircraft conduct mutual operations to improve warfighting skills. In this case, there were fifty-six ships, eight submarines, two hundred twenty aircraft, and more than twenty-seven thousand military personnel skirmishing in the Hawaiian operational area.

Three weeks earlier, as we prepared to leave Japan for Hawaii, I addressed two hanging chads from my meeting with Admiral Blacker. Did I take as orders his *suggestions* to discard both our red balls caps and our red dog? Not exactly.... Our policy of wearing red ball caps only when at sea had met the Admiral's requirement, if not his intent. As to Jenna, I decided to keep her on board until someone formally ordered her removal.

Of course, if that happened, *my* removal was also probable.

I took the risk.

Jenna had quickly become an integral part of the crew, improving morale and pride more than I could have imagined. She had become more than a mascot— she was now the ship's *icon*.

Vandy joined a Japanese task force for several months to participate in RIMPAC. We sailed from Japan to Hawaii with four Japan Maritime Self-Defense Force (JMSDF) ships. I took orders from Rear Admiral Yoshihiro Sakaue, the commander of JMSDF Escort Flotilla One, during this trip. He expected his ships to be flawless and was not hesitant to provide immediate and blunt feedback when that was not the case. The Japanese Navy is precise and thorough in every manner, and we learned from them. And, in the end, they learned a few things from us.

Lesson 1 was on refueling.

Our ability to take on fuel and provisions while at sea—called UNREP for underway replenishment—enables the Navy to be a global force that can remain indefinitely off any shore. We don't need overflight rights or a base to operate from, affording the President to have military or humanitarian options independent of foreign support. UNREP is a dangerous, exacting evolution. A ship pulls up beside a replenishment ship ("oiler") that pumps thousands of gallons of fuel through huge hoses stretched across 150 feet of water.

Jenna was not allowed onto the main deck during UNREPs, where tensioned wires, lines, rigs, and busy sailors in steel-toed boots put her at high risk. She watched from the O3 level, the same level as the bridge and well above the fray. She extended her head between the lifelines to oversee the proceedings below, head bowed like Snoopy on his doghouse. She observed carefully, silent and inscrutable, moving from one vantage point to another to find the best view.

Occasionally a sailor looked up and greeted Jenna, but the real treat was watching the people on the oiler. Amazement, confusion, pointing, waving, grins...even at 150 feet I could see that each person was seeing something new and unexpected during this Kabuki dance of big gray ships. Often the master of the oiler, a salty mariner who had hundreds or thousands of these evolutions under his belt, called over to ask about the red dog roaming our upper decks. And so the story of our special shipmate grew from grassroots, passed on by

NEAL J. KUSUMOTO, CAPTAIN, US NAVY (RET)

word of mouth between mariners in smoky waterfront dives, each enhancing the story *just a little*.

We were confident as we began our first refueling with the Japanese Navy. *Vandy* had done this many times, and the crew was very proficient. But I quickly realized that we had on hiking boots to conduct this difficult evolution, while they showed up with running shoes and stopwatches. No, really, they had stopwatches. Our approach and hookup, at twenty-five knots and quick by US standards, was glacial compared to theirs. On the Japanese ships it was a whirl of organized chaos: sailors in matching coveralls, hand flags waving and whistles blowing to control each step, sailors sprinting from one area to the next. From our vantage point they looked like army ants moving at hyper speed, a model of efficiency and precision.

It was a race, and no one had told us.

Later that day the Admiral transmitted a message listing how long it took each ship to refuel. We were dead last, far behind the pack.

We adapted to the JMSDF model and practiced. The crew took on the challenge, always wanting to be the best and understanding the combat necessity to do so. At first tension was high, and our pace remained slow as we stumbled to make haste. But in a few weeks, we went from awkward kid running a lap in canvas tennis shoes and black socks to an Olympic sprinter. By the time we got to Hawaii we were competitive with the Japanese track stars.

And no doubt the best in the US Navy.

Dan stood ramrod straight on the bridge wing, clad in his clan's colors, piping an ancient song that blasted over the loudspeakers as we prepared to detach from an oiler. He was playing our "breakaway song," the only time Navy ships incorporate music into our naval routine. The breakaway was the fun part of refueling at sea, when the stress of a dangerous evolution was gone, and we kicked the *Vandy* to flank speed to show off our seagoing muscle car. Every ship has a breakaway song that they play over the loudspeakers. Some ships play the same one for an entire year, some change songs every evolution. The breakaway song boosts our mood, adds a soundtrack to our memories, and pumps us up. Most ships blast rock and roll, but this crew was proud to be different, to have live music, to be linked to fierce highland fighters. Dan was an accomplished player who practiced his Irish heritage standing on steel instead of moss, looking across the blue Pacific rather than rolling green hills. Like Jenna, bagpipes were unique. I had never seen bagpipes on a ship before and have never seen them since.

Of course, I had never heard of a dog on a ship either.

As I sat in my chair on the starboard bridge wing, I felt the ship surge forward as we came up to flank speed, heard the gas turbines winding up, and watched the oiler quickly drop back. Jenna came forward from her amidships vantage point, the wind whipping the hair on top of her head. Dan played on, his cheeks glowing with effort as he tried to match the volume of the ship's roaring engines. I stole a quick glance inside the bridge and smiled. Everyone was grinning and enjoying the release of tension as we raced ahead, leaving the oiler with nothing more than the lilting melody of the moors. We turned to port with a standard rudder (fifteen degrees), heeling over because of our speed, like leaning into a curve on a bicycle. I looked down.

Jenna was sitting below me, relaxed and leaning her upper body into the curve. Her eyes were squinted, her nose extended just through the lifeline. Was she enjoying Dan's music? Hard to tell, but she was enjoying the stiff wind we were generating.

The final ten days of RIMPAC were the "tactical" phase, when the gloves came off. Training and collaboration were done; it was time to start the wartime scenario. Although no actual weapons were fired, the ships, jets, and submarines simulated a battle at sea. A frigate was one of the little guys, smaller than the cruisers, aircraft carriers, and destroyers...even smaller than many submarines. But the *Vandy* was a *big dog in a small package*, and like Jenna, we weren't about to bow to anyone...no matter what size they were.

We went into the fight with a chip on our shoulder. We had been working hard to get our teamwork and systems in top working order, much like we polished our UNREP skills. We were cruising off the coast of Maui when the war game began. I addressed the crew from the bridge microphone, providing a brief synopsis of the scenario and our role. I did this at least once a day, knowing that most of the crew was below decks with no idea what was going on, no way to know how we were doing, no way to understand how their work contributed to our ability to fight.

After I finished, I held the mike as Dan piped a battle tune that reached every area of the ship. The trilling melody transported us to misty moors, the pipes wailing of dampness rising from green heaths and strong men rising to defend their homes. First used as a call to battle, the pipes have stirred warriors for centuries. On *Vandy*, far from any moor or even land, the mystical piping wafted above the ship's mechanical drone, adding a powerful sense of purpose. Although the shots in this fight were simulated, this would be a true test of our tactical capability.

As the ship surged forward, our blood also surged and our sinews flexed in readiness to meet our foes. Even Jenna's blood ran hotter as she paced from bridge wing to bridge wing. We had been at quiet ship, minimizing the sound we put into the water that a submarine might detect, and keeping radars and radios silent. Now we took the offensive, blazing into the strait between Maui and Lanai at twenty-five knots. We passed within four miles of Lahaina, with Haleakala Crater glowing red from the setting sun. Speed was one of our assets, but it also identified *Vandy* as a warship.

The world was tinged in cool shades of blue, a harmonious blended horizon that ranged from sky blue to deep sea blue. Twilight is that magical thirty to sixty minutes when everything takes on a bluish hue. The sun was below the horizon, but there was still enough light to be able to see. The lack of direct sunlight eliminated shadows and silhouetted the islands before us. We could still make out the horizon, yet also distinguish the brightest planets and stars while in this twilight zone. From a warfighting perspective, twilight provided enough illumination to coordinate an attack yet enough shadow to delay discovery. We were using this transition period to our advantage, hoping to find our foe's minds wandering as they drank in the captivating transition from day to night.

Vandy was *forthright and bold*, living up to the Shiba Inu standard. We struck fast, withdrew, hid, then re-attacked. Lethal and accurate, we turned the seas red with our enemy's blood (also simulated). We located and sank three enemy ships using surface-to-surface missiles, all without getting hit ourselves. We also displayed our anti-air warfare credentials, shooting down two enemy jets with surface-to-air missiles. All simulated, of course, but judged by a team of experts running the exercise. The coup de grâce was sinking a submarine, the only one sunk during the entire monthlong exercise.

At the end of this complex exercise *Vandegrift* had excelled above, on, and below the sea, notching more kills than any other ship. Admiral Sakaue presented a plaque as the *Best Warfighter in RIMPAC* to us. We had just played in the Super Bowl of naval exercises and come home with the trophy. We were justifiably proud but also understood that even the most complex exercise could not compare to real battle. What we had not felt was real fear, as we were never in danger of losing the ship or our lives.

While we had fun times, that is not the norm. Navy sailors are standing watch in every ocean across the world as you read this. They are unsung heroes who make monumental sacrifices so we can sleep well at night. They spend six...seven...eight...nine months away from home and loved ones, missing births and deaths, birthdays and holidays, becoming a stranger to those at home. They sleep on a small rack, with one small locker to hold all their belongings, in a space shared with eighty-one shipmates, with no windows, no privacy, no choosing where or with whom they live, eating whatever is served, doing whatever they are told. Digging deep to keep turning and burning through long days at sea, finding something extra to stay alert in that elongated fifth hour of watch, fixing a piece of gear, again, without complaint. Does this sound like prison? Prisoners don't work nearly this hard. There is little slack time and little time for frivolity. Sailors work on a gray ship, wearing the same uniform as everyone else, often in brutally hot or cold conditions, grinding through wearisome jobs interspersed with dangerous evolutions. And they don't have a dog to boost their spirits, like we did.

Whoever can bear this life, whoever can prosper and grow in this alien environment, whoever can lead others with the few tools given...is special. These sailors are the lifeblood of the Navy. They serve their country not only through battlefield heroics but by employing incredible stamina and strength to pull their ships through every test. Inane administrative requirements, low pay, long hours, antique equipment, working and living conditions that would be unacceptable in any prison...none of it detours these heroic grinders.

Our bond was forged in a life together at sea, packed tightly for many months, night and day, work and play, facing and overcoming challenges as a crew...and winning as a team. This bond remains strong today, more than two decades later. Life has gone on; all but a few are long gone from the Navy. We have experienced marriages, births and deaths, divorces, job changes...yet the crew would come together if a shipmate needed help.

The sun balanced just above a tranquil sea as we sailed back to Pearl Harbor. The crew congregated outside to wonder at the glorious display and to celebrate our RIMPAC victory. Dan sometimes played during twilight, his lilting melody adding another dimension to the incredible scene, transcribing a small video file onto our brains. We watched for the green flash after the last vestige of sun disappeared, bonded by shared experiences we would treasure for the rest of our lives.

Jenna was always on the weather decks during evening twilight, maintaining the same rotation as her shipmates. The measured click of her nails on the non-skid announced her unhurried arrival on the bridge wing. She made one pass through the bridge, scanning each person but not making eye contact. She then returned to her spot on the starboard bridge wing and sat, muzzle extended through the lifelines, eyes slit as her nose twitched. She was appreciating a myriad layer of smells, cataloging them by time and source. It must have been quite an odorous panorama; she sat for hours breathing it in. Darkness drove everyone but the lookouts inside, nothing more to see. But Jenna lingered, her nose connected to the scent data stream of the night.

As we approached Oahu to enter port, we were informed that customs wanted to see Jenna when they came aboard for their inspection. This was normally a perfunctory check for Navy warships, since they knew we weren't smuggling dope or contraband.

How did they know about Jenna?

I was concerned as we approached my home island. Hawaii had strict quarantine laws to prevent rabies from spreading to the islands, including a 120-day mandatory kennel incarceration for all pets entering the state. As I sat in my chair on the bridge wing, pondering how flying fish stayed in the air so long, I considered possible outcomes of the customs visit. The options seemed to be that Jenna would have to go into quarantine, far from our care, whenever we entered Hawaii.

Or we could not enter port.

My concern grew to mild alarm. The crew loved Jenna, but did they love her more than their treasured Hawaiian port visits? As we got closer, everyone who was not on watch lined the rails to get a glimpse of the island as we waited offshore for our turn to enter port. We were close enough to smell the tropical flowers, to see trimarans conducting sunset cruises, and to watch surfers riding the waves off Waikiki. The crew could smell good liberty like Jenna could smell a hamburger being grilled, and they sniffed good times dead ahead.

There was even a marriage planned.

I paced in my cabin, which meant taking three steps then doing an about-face. Most of the crew loved Jenna, but all of the crew loved liberty. Especially in Hawaii. Jenna was liable to take an unexpected plunge off the ship late one night, aided by a distraught sailor.

The chiefs, always resourceful, found a possible loophole. They had uncovered an old codicil, left over from World War II, during their initial research to find rules that banned dogs on ships. This elderly document provided special dispensation to mascots, prevalent on Navy ships back then, to enter Pearl Harbor. This was nothing that would stand up in court, but it provided some faint hope.

Customs boarded wearing aloha shirts and big smiles. I talked *da kine*—pidgin English—with them for a few minutes to establish rapport. I was surprised to find that my collar was damp. From the humidity? Wait, we were inside the air-conditioned wardroom. So much for never letting them see me sweat.

The XO got through the routine paperwork, and it looked like they were ready to leave. But just as my heart started to slow, the head agent looked over and asked, "It's true, you guys gt one dog?"

I was on the verge of lying, doing whatever was needed to keep Jenna on board. It would have been so easy. I looked at their smiling, expectant faces.

"Yeah, brah, foh sure. You like see her?"

Smiles widened, and two inspectors even waggled *shaka* thumb-pinkie signs at one another.

"Foh real? I neva knew one ship with da kine dog."

I released the breath that I had been holding for...how long?

Jenna was ushered in, sleepy-eyed and ruffled. The lead agent clapped his hands together into a steeple and brought them to his chest, fingers aimed towards his grin. He turned to the others and exchanged high fives. Jenna ambled over when I called her, eyeing the visitors and somewhat politely sniffing proffered fingers. The agents ran their hands along her back as she drowsily passed. She sauntered over and jumped up on the couch. Social time was over.

But it was enough. The agents departed, smiles blazing and buzzing about *da kine dog.*

Although we dodged the quarantine bullet, I got news with much worse implications. Big news, big implications. Admiral Blacker was getting promoted. My mind raced as I considered the consequences. Although he would leave his post in Japan right after we returned from RIMPAC, he would remain in our chain of command...just further up the chain. I could still feel his eyes burning into me, still feel my heart drop as he scorned our red ball caps.

And then there was that other red line he had drawn. Jenna.

Surely he would be buried under too many import-ant matters to worry about little ole us. We were small fry, too small to even bother frying.

His eyes, dark and unblinking. I could hear the crackle of hot oil and feel the sear from the frying pan. He would not be one to forget...or to forgive.

We had not yet crossed a red line. I could still change course and unload our red contraband in Hawaii.

I tossed and turned that night. And the next. What was best for the ship...for the crew...for me? As much as I believed I made decisions thinking of the crew first, I did not want to jettison my own career. A stray dog and red ball caps were symbols of *Vandy* pride, but were they important to the ship's readiness and morale? As I turned over for the umpteenth time, I looked over at Jenna asleep on her couch.

No bad dreams there, she snoozed without a care.

I flashed back to all the smiles and laughs that Jenna initiated every day, far more than normal on a busy Navy ship. I heard the laughter and felt the joy, felt the warm blanket of camaraderie.

I decided to stay on course.

I knew this decision was right for the ship; the uncer-tainty was whether I would be ordered to a desk job in some Navy backwater. I turned over and was instantly asleep, awaking refreshed to the sound of Jenna yawn-ing more loudly than necessary. Her signal that it was time to let her out.

10.

AHOY *KITTY*

Everyone must row with the oars he has.

— Dutch proverb

had to break the crew's hearts. We had one last port visit in Hawaii, and we thirsted for liberty as only sailors who have been at sea can. Dreams of Hawaiian adventures played in high definition. We were basking in the warmth of our glorious RIMPAC performance, ecstatic to be the Most Valuable Player and looking forward to celebrating in Honolulu before heading back to Japan. RIMPAC was a monthlong exercise broken into several parts, and *Vandy* had berthed in Pearl Harbor in between those segments.

A day before entering port for our final visit, the unthinkable happened. The cruiser that was designated to stay at sea accompanying the aircraft carrier *Kitty Hawk* suffered a casualty that required her to return to Pearl Harbor for repairs. We were ordered to take their place as the carrier's escort because I was the most junior commanding officer in RIMPAC. As visions of palm trees and mai tais faded to black, our noses twitched like Jenna's as we picked up a rotten odor. Had that cruiser just flopped like a soccer player, feigning injury to get a few more days in Hawaii? Somehow we were being penalized for that illusory foul. Besides missing our final liberty and a chance to bond with our international naval brethren, we would also be unable to refuel in port. That meant we would get a rare *opportunity* to refuel from the aircraft carrier.

A rare, tense, tedious opportunity to be fastened to a monstrous ship.

At a distance of 150 feet.

For many hours.

Imagine driving your car on the highway for hours, pacing a big rig beside you that has a tensioned steel cable hooked to your car. And there is no concrete divider to prevent head-on collisions.

Captain "Black Jack" Samar, Commanding Officer of *Kitty Hawk*, was a fighter pilot with a distinguished record. These guys have nerves of steel; I saw the movie *Top Gun*. It took a lot to make Black Jack nervous, but nervous he was. *Kitty Hawk* had not conducted an UNREP in many years, so the crew was untrained and their gear in disrepair. He called me several times in the days prior to refueling to go over the evolution and to ensure we were prepared. Most of all he wanted to gauge whether I knew what I was doing, or if he would be putting his ship at risk.

My reply: *We got this!*

But the stress from the captain of the *Kitty Hawk* spread to us, their anxiety an airborne virus that tightened the muscles in our necks and dried our throats. Instead of a standard replenishment at sea, this one took on a different tone, which was *not* a good thing. I also knew that any glitch would rise to Admiral Blacker's attention, presenting a justifiable reason to fire me. We were always careful during these dangerous operations, briefing the evolution and possible problems well ahead of time. We had learned from the Japanese Navy that slow does not mean safe. Being ultracareful meant a protracted evolution with more time alongside, which increased the risk of an accident. We needed to be loose, but there was no time to do twenty-five jumping jacks or wind sprints to settle our nerves.

Dangerous waters were dead ahead.

Our newfound replenishment proficiency was mismatched with the carrier's multiyear fueling hiatus... like a NASCAR driver pulling into a local service station expecting to get fuel and new tires in fifteen seconds.

I got on the 1MC announcing system. "Good morning, *Vandegrift*, this is the captain. As you know, we are making final preps to receive fuel from the *Kitty Hawk* so we can stay out here to provide escort services."

Tittering on the bridge. I shook my head but could not suppress a smile.

"Not *that* kind of escort service, get your minds out of the gutter. The *Kitty Hawk* has not done this in years, so it may take longer than normal, and we may need to make changes on the fly. We're good at this, probably the best in the fleet. Keep your head in the game and don't lose focus, no matter how long this takes. Let's show them how *Vandy* does business."

It was a beautiful Hawaiian day, the kind illustrated on tourism websites. Wispy clouds tumbled at high altitudes, highlighting the bright blue sky. A light breeze humidly washed across our faces as we examined the aircraft carrier a couple of miles ahead. I leaned from the captain's chair, looking over the side. The sea was unruffled by waves or wind, contrails from flying fish the only imperfection to the blue expanse. Jenna watched the flying fish with interest; I had to admit that it was hard not to watch them scatter from our threatening bow wave. Some flew long and straight, some went for short flights, each one different. The perfect surroundings diffused my stress. I scanned the horizon; not another ship within the twelve-mile arc of my vision. Pushing out of my chair, I wandered over to a radar repeater. No ships close to us. The tone on the bridge was light, everyone relaxed but alert. I had Jenna taken down to the wardroom where she was safe from harm.

And out of sight.

We set the replenishment detail. Seaman Chris Mirabella was at my elbow with sound-powered telephones strapped to his chest, earmuff headsets clamped so tightly to his head that he had to periodically pull them off to allow blood flow. Chris was a cocky, sardonic, and smart young Californian with a New Jersey attitude. He had been advanced to petty officer twice, then promptly demoted twice after doing something stupid. He clearly felt superior to some of his "superiors." Although he was smarter than most, his antipathy did not endear him to those trying to get work out of him. He was a smart aleck, like me, and my main communications link for maneuvering evolutions.

The Navy has exact terminology to ensure everyone knows precisely what each command means. One misunderstood command could lead to disaster. Chris knew what I was going to say, repeating the exact wording for anchoring, mooring, or UNREPs. He just did not have the experience and judgment to determine *when* to order each step. He even prompted me if he thought I had missed something. Not saying he was ready to be the captain, but we could have done worse.

The guys up forward on the forecastle (pronounced "foke-sil") were setting up the phone and distance line, a nylon line to be passed to the *Kitty Hawk* and then hand-tended. This line had flags at twenty-foot intervals, the flag colors alternated in a green-red-yellow-blue-white-green pattern so we could determine the distance between ships. I can still remember the order of colors today because of the brain-sticking mnemonic "Go Rub Your Balls With Grease"—just try to forget that—which corresponded to the first letter of each color. Before you get your, ah, testicles in a bunch...the *balls* referenced are those mounted on both sides of the magnetic compass to keep it true. This line also included our sound-powered phone cable so I could speak to my counterpart on the other ship. Sound a bit antique compared to laser range finders and VHF walkie-talkies? Perhaps, but this system worked in any visibility without transmitting signals that could be detected or intercepted.

I turned my gaze aft to observe the main effort. The boatswain's mates, led by First Class Petty Officer Tom Hengel, were setting up to receive the fueling rig. Tom, grizzled at thirty, was an accomplished leader. Rugged good looks, with a dry smile and quick wit, he had just met his future wife during our port visit in Honolulu. He was not ecstatic about being extended at sea instead of spending a few precious days with her during that breathtaking time when love is first unfolding. The wild and crazy types were in Tom's deck division, where all the undesignated (too new to have a rating specialty) sailors resided. These "deck apes" did the dangerous jobs involving tensioned steel wires, small boats in big waves, and working underneath hovering helicopters. They also did the most tedious jobs, like chipping paint from the hull and decks...then painting...then repeating forevermore to counter the never-ending rust. To lead these guys, you had to be a strong alpha personality and know your shit cold.

The crew was decked out in life jackets, hard hats, steel-toed shoes, and attached lights so we had a chance of finding someone should he fall overboard. Pants and shirts were tucked in to minimize the chance of being snagged by the rigging, which was a thick steel rope that tensioned to fifteen hundred pounds.

Fifteen hundred pounds is enough to pull your house off of its foundation.

Fifteen hundred pounds is enough to cut through metal hulls or rip apart human bodies.

I turned to look above me. Signalman Ryan "Rhino" Phillips was flashing Morse code with a two-foot-diameter signal light; the intermittent rapid clicking of the shutters as they opened and closed sounded like an old-time teletype. He communicated at lightning speed with his counterpart on the *Kitty Hawk*, and I didn't even try to follow along. Rhino flashed me a quick grin as he continued his visual wireless communications. He was full of energy, ready to work hard or lead the way on liberty, equal parts youthful impetuosity and maturing work ethic.

We lined up the *Vandy* a mile behind the carrier. The huge gray ship blocked much of the horizon ahead of us, even at this distance. *Kitty Hawk* left a long trail like some giant sea slug, her huge propellers churning the blue water into white-green foam. Rhino hoisted the Romeo flag on the mast to indicate we were ready to make our approach. A flag on the *Kitty Hawk*'s starboard side was "closed up" to the top of the mast, and the Officer of the Deck told me we had permission to make our approach. All stations were prepared—I gave him the thumbs up.

It was show time.

My boss, Commodore Ferguson, was watching from the *Kitty Hawk* flag bridge with his captain peers. And with *his* boss, Rear Admiral Keating. Black Jack was pacing the bridge trying to speed the glacial proceedings, wishing it was already over. It would have been wise to ease our way in, to take the guesswork out of it, to let everyone relax and take a deep breath. But that was not our style.

All Ahead Full!

We were coming in at twenty-five knots, coming in hot as if this were a real wartime scenario. This was the ship version of a fighter jet landing on the flight deck, only we didn't have a wire to stop us. The engineers had the ship purring, and the bow surged ahead as the gas turbines wound up and the propeller dug in. We quickly made up the ground, maneuvering to 120 feet lateral distance. As our bow passed the carrier's stern, I ordered twelve knots to match her speed. We slid into place as we decelerated, so close it seemed like her aircraft elevators would overhang our deck. They passed over the wire line and tensioned it once we had it secured. Although my shoulders were hunched with stress, I willed myself to sit in my chair on the port side, feet propped up, watching silently.

It was a perfect approach...the last perfect part of this precarious evolution.

I glanced astern. The deck crew was at ease in ranks, rocking on their heels in the slight seas while gazing at the aircraft carrier that was close enough to hear their voices, waiting to spring to action. I looked across the water at the carrier's refueling crew, who were on a small platform. Actually, it just appeared small against the backdrop of the enormous carrier. There was lots of movement, three sailors tugging a line attached to the rig and others scurrying about the platform. The sharp percussion of steel-on-steel hammering rose above the shouts of their boatswain's mates. Despite all the frantic action, the refueling rig did not move. It appeared that some of the steel wires were crossed.

We waited.

Black Jack called to inform me that they were having some difficulties with their rig, and they expected to have it ready soon. A sunny day with little cloud cover turned into a detriment as the crew baked in long pants, long-sleeved shirts, and plastic hard hats. After thirty minutes, with no discernible progress in getting things sorted out, I put our crew at ease. We rotated people out of formation to spend time in the shade and to hydrate, since it might be a long day. I was less concerned about how we looked to those above than I was with the welfare of my crew, and since I had a good chain of command, I didn't worry about appearance. Didn't worry too much, anyway.

As I stewed in my chair, I began to look at what was going on around me. And began to wonder if perhaps we might be a bit *too* loose. We must have looked like Barbary pirates to the two levels of my chain of command observing from above. We had started a beard-growing

NEAL J. KUSUMOTO, CAPTAIN, US NAVY (RET)

contest when I found out we were not returning to Pearl Harbor for the last few days of the RIMPAC celebration. The Navy was clean shaven, so the ability to grow a beard was limited to weekends and while on leave. This contest allowed the guys to grow beards without spousal sanction, compare them daily, and tease each other. It was a minor compensation for sailors who had lost their treasured Hawaiian liberty and had only a long transit back to Japan to look forward to. We were a few days into this contest, which meant my "beard" was unnoticeable unless someone was standing next to me in bright sunlight. But many of these guys looked like they had just moseyed down from the Ozarks. Beard-growing contests were not unheard of on small ships, but I doubted if they were held on aircraft carriers with Admirals embarked.

Another "lucky" detail was that we had designated one day of the week during long periods at sea as "hat day," when the crew was allowed to wear civilian hats rather than their red ball caps. Adding an informal piece of home to a strict uniform was an easy way to cheer people up and let them forget that they had to spend eight to twelve hours on watch day in and day out.

Yes, it also happened to be hat day.

Some wore football team ball caps or other modest coverings. But many hats were less discreet. Fedoras, upturned black pirate hats embroidered with skull and crossbones, tall drooping Cat-in-the-Hats, cowboy hats both garish and traditional. It was Halloween on each sailor's head. I never saw these guys wearing this crazy stuff while ashore on liberty.

I sat in my chair, swiveling to survey the replenishment rig, the carrier, and the surreal scene around me. I had mixed feelings as I imagined what the folks observing us from above must be thinking. Is he running a pirate ship? The coincidental confluence of events was rotten timing, anti-feng shui, bad juju. As I sat in the sun with my thoughts, I heard the clitter of long nails on the non-skid deck.

Jenna emerged, rested and curious, to roam the deck amid pirates and cavemen. She nosed between the lifelines, eyeing the large ship beside us, sniffing the sea breeze yet unsullied by petroleum fumes. Her red coat shined, the arched golden-blond feathers of her tail fluffed by twelve knots of relative wind. I wondered what she was thinking as she gazed at the gray leviathan, human ants scurrying about the decks, an invisible stream of smells wafting from the aircraft carrier. This was the maritime version of your dog gazing out the car window, snuffling the breeze, enjoying the visual and olfactory views.

Jenna turned away, mild interest satisfied, and trotted around her patch of the ship. She checked out her mates working at various tasks, walking the perimeter slowly. The non-skid must have been hot, but she didn't seem to mind, her pads toughened to the rough material and heat.

Of course, looking went both ways. Rhino got a semaphore message, "You have a fucking dog onboard?" I found out many years later that this missive was one of many he traded trying to get a date with a female signalman. We also got an electronic note from the *Kitty Hawk* asking the same rhetorical question, "You guys have a dog?" Clearly the word had spread quickly, even the people working in the center of the aircraft carrier knew of Jenna.

I could only smile, feeling proud and a little sick at the same time.

We were alongside *Kitty Hawk* for seven hours. Seven l-o-n-g hours in the shadow of this massive ship, taking on fuel drip by drip. Normally we refueled from an oiler in less than an hour. We stayed alongside until the sun set, and even then didn't get all the fuel we wanted. Navy ships don't routinely refuel in the dark because we need to be able to spot fuel leaking into the water, and with their old rig that was a distinct possibility.

Seven hours alongside.

Seven hours to worry about the risk of smashing into the side of the aircraft carrier, seven hours to worry about the impression I was making with my chain of command. Bad enough that Admiral Blacker thought we were rogue...I didn't need other senior officers having the same opinion. Sitting on the bridge wing should have been relaxing, but I was trying hard not to clench my teeth.

I looked down. Jenna had returned from her tour of the deck and was sitting a few feet away. She was stock-still, relaxed, only her nose quivering occasionally. I sat back in my chair and leaned my head against the headrest. I closed my eyes and took deep, even breaths through my nose and expelled the air through my mouth. Unlike Jenna, I could not make my nose quiver. At first, nothing. But after a few minutes the steady background noise of the ship faded, and my shoulders relaxed (I had not realized they were hunched). I smelled the salty air, a briny almost-fishy aroma. Like the smell at a marina, only lighter and fresher. I focused on breathing in by expanding my stomach and exhaling while pushing in with my stomach, relaxing me further. Still aware of my surroundings, but somehow detached.

And then it hit me. The distinctive odor of...marine varnish? My mind switched back to *now* as I wondered when the quartermasters had been preserving the railing. I opened my eyes, still relaxed but now back in the world of vision. I looked down at Jenna, who sat in a trance-like state. Dogs can sense so much more through their noses than we can. She must have been experiencing the odoriferous version of a beautiful sunset. I wondered whether she could extract the overwhelming varnish aroma so it did not tarnish the full bouquet. Or did she enjoy that smell too?

We disconnected the rig as the sun was dipping into the ocean ahead of us, its rays imparting an orange glow to weary faces. As the ship accelerated away from the aircraft carrier, we watched silently as the sun's edge blinked out beneath the earth's arc.

It wasn't long before the *Vandy* Boyz hooked up with *Kitty Hawk* sailors again, though this time there wasn't 120 feet of ocean separating them. And all of them were fully fueled and ready for action.

Quincy Williams told me of the Christmas Eve brawl many years after it happened. Quincy became an actor in Hollywood after his Navy career, smooth and polished in his looks, speech, and actions. He assured me he has not Hollywoodized this story, that it is as accurate as it can be these many years and beers later. Sailors have been portrayed in movies and television as hard-drinking characters, ready to fight or to romance at the drop of a hat (or skirt). Movies must have drama and interesting characters, and typecasting sailors and other social groups makes it easier to build a scene that is easy to digest. I would like to protest on the behalf of sailors everywhere...except there is some basis for that stereotype.

Club Alliance, known as the "A Club," was the bar on base in Japan where enlisted sailors went to drink and to meet local girls. Mixing cheap alcohol, eighteen- to twenty-year-old male hormones, too few women, and rivalries between ships was a recipe for conflict. A group of *Kitty Hawk* thugs started harassing seven *Vandy* sailors—perfect angels, of course—in the club. Words were exchanged but nothing more because the remote chance of meeting a girl trumped macho pride. But when the club closed, everyone gathered outside, where punches were thrown. At this point the sides were about even. Security was nearby, so the groups parted...to find a more remote location.

When they met again that night, on a desolate hill near the base hospital, a full-scale brawl erupted. But the *Vandy* Boyz had been ambushed! A large crowd of carrier bangers were waiting. The boys held their own but were fortunate that police cars arrived, scattering everyone like sardines fleeing a porpoise. Each crew member took a different route back to the ship, where they met on the mess decks to ensure everyone had made it back. They survived with scrapes, bruises, and stories to tell.

11.

THE DOG WATCH

Control of the seas can mean peace.
Control of the seas can mean victory.
The United States must control the seas
if it is to protect your security.

— PRESIDENT JOHN F. KENNEDY

Nights at sea were often like driving your car down a deserted freeway at midnight: dark, monotonous, each minute dawdling. But nights could also be enchanting. Standing on the bridge wing, I was mesmerized watching the bow wave generate a green phosphorescent glow as millions of minuscule plankton lit up, alarmed by our unexpected intrusion. The only sound was the steady swish of the hull cutting through a dark and silent ocean. The moon and stars burst from a sky unmuted by artificial lights, no smog to dim their radiance. There were countless stars, sharp pinholes in a vast black canopy, their collective glow painting the ship and sea a ghostly pallor. Sirius, the Dog Star, beckoned across galaxies to Jenna. The moon sent a path of golden luster across the waters, never wavering, a searchlight that tracked our every move.

But those standing watch could not be lulled by the serene beauty of the ocean. It was hard to take even a few minutes to appreciate the splendor, no matter how tranquil the conditions. Sailors then and now work in sickness and in health. In freezing rain, snow, high winds, rough seas, searing heat, and liquid humidity. They don't even get a break if they are seasick, and many turn green when it gets rough. Sailors just hang a plastic barf bag from their back pockets and continue to stand watch or perform their "day jobs."

Fortunately, Jenna was impervious to the rise and fall of the ship, even in high seas. She quickly mastered the art of timing the roll of the ship, using her four legs like pneumatic pistons to keep her balance. If it got too rough, she reluctantly abandoned her favorite spot on the bridge wing and retired inside to the small chart room. The watch team would place a small blanket on the deck for her and ensure there was nothing adrift that might slide around.

Jenna *did* mind when chairs and other unsecured items wandered, threatening to crash into her. She discovered stable sanctuaries, those pieces of furniture that were welded or screwed to the deck. In rough weather she could be found rolled into a ball at the end of the wardroom couch, still except for her dark eyes following the suddenly traitorous chairs that danced across the deck. I sought her out when seas were high and took her to my cabin, which had fixed couches and little besides a pen or two that might slide around.

As you read this, sailors are standing watch on every US Navy ship in the world. They are qualified to ensure that the ship operates safely, whether at sea or in port. It takes many watch standers to run the engineering plant, operate the weapons systems, navigate the ship, and communicate with other ships. Everyone works twelve- to eighteen-hour days at sea, often doing hard, dirty, hot work. A frigate has twenty-one people standing watch during peacetime steaming. Sailors stand eight to twelve hours of watch a day and also perform their "day jobs." The *dog watch* was our favorite. It does not refer to someone who watches over Jenna but rather a way to split the evening watch so all watch standers can eat dinner. The first dog watch is the period between 4:00 and 6:00 p.m., and the second is between 6:00 and 8:00 p.m. Dog watches also rotate watch standers so that the sleepy/dark/cold mid-watch (midnight to 4:00 a.m.) is equally shared. No one knows the origin of the term "dog watch," though it has been used since the seventeenth century.

Jenna, though curious to explore new places on the ship, generally avoided the engineering spaces. Too hot, too loud, too cramped, too malodorous, too many ladders to climb down. But she loved the engineers and bonded with them. Engineers are a special breed, sled dogs who work in a harsh environment. Crawling in the bilges to clean pockets of brackish water, squirming through tight spaces beneath steaming-rotating machinery. Sweating through long-sleeved coveralls in ninety- to one-hundred-degree temperatures and molten humidity while repairing engines, generators, and other machinery.

A junior engineer would climb up four sets of stairs, find Jenna, and lug her down to their control station. It was hot there, but less noisy and sufferable compared to the main spaces below. I would find her standing on the large table in the middle of the control room, surrounded by hardened men in grimy coveralls and sporting wide grins while taking turns petting her. Each carefully wiped his rough and grimy hands on a rag, then gently stroked her a few times. Jenna, a loner, held her tail at half-mast. She liked the engineers and was willing to put up with more attention than usual.

Jenna wandered the ship at will, visiting watch standers as she made her rounds. Who knew what kind of snack they might have hidden in their pockets? I would find her sitting with, but not *too* near, the after-lookout on the fantail contemplating the ship's wake. Staring at the ship's path of white and green churned water was mesmerizing, inducing a state of semi-consciousness where minds might wander anywhere in the world. Was Jenna thinking of her next meal or her last port visit? Or was she just spacing out?

I presumed that *even red dogs had odd daydreams*.

We also stood watches while in port, every hour of every day. The OOD oversaw two watch standers on the quarterdeck, the area where crew and visitors enter and exit the ship. You already know that Jenna exited the ship here, often without permission and not following naval protocol. Other watch standers included a sounding and security watch that checked for flooding and fires, an armed security rover, a pier watch, and a communications watch. A large portion of the crew stayed on board when in port to respond to emergencies and to keep the ship secure. Normally we had four duty sections, which meant that each sailor spent every fourth night on board standing watch or standing by to fight a fire or an intruder. There was no overtime or compensation for these "duty days" when sailors spent weekends and weeknights on the ship, even when in home port. Today's sailors maintain much the same rotation.

The Command Duty Officer (CDO) was in charge of the ship when the XO and I were ashore. I had to have full trust and confidence in this officer's judgment and decision-making, as he must be able to make critical on-the-spot decisions. He might have to deal with someone seeking political asylum; a US ship is a piece of the United States, no matter where she is. He must decide whether the threat to the ship or crew warrants a "shoot to kill" response. The CDO becomes even more vital when the ship is anchored. The ship could drag or break away from the anchor, be struck by a passing ship, or be attacked. The CDO may have to get the ship underway with a skeleton crew and maneuver in restricted waters. There are many more scenarios, most of which are unlikely. But they can, and do, happen.

This scenario came into play in Phuket, Thailand. Because of seasonal weather patterns, we had to anchor on the seaward side of the cape rather than near the harbor and bus the crew across the peninsula to town. Conditions upon arrival were mild, negligible wind and current, and we were alone in the anchorage. After we secured the ship, I got into one of the water taxis and went ashore with the XO and other officers.

We were in my sedan on the trek across the peninsula for only five minutes when my three-pound mobile phone—think of a handheld walkie-talkie seen in old army movies—rang. J. R., the CDO, was breathless. I could hear his heart pounding over the phone, or so it seemed.

"Captain, the ship is dragging anchor! We've taken several fixes and are outside of the drag circle!"

The drag circle is the radius in which the ship swings based upon the length of anchor chain let out. The weight of the chain, rather than the anchor itself, holds a ship in place. We had seventy fathoms, or 420 feet, of heavy chain lying on the bottom. I looked out the rear window at the ship, five miles away and opening. Skies were blue and the wind was light. Dragging the anchor seemed unlikely. "J. R., take a deep breath. Is the anchor chain bouncing?" Bouncing would indicate that the anchor was lifting off the ground periodically.

"N-nooo sir...not that I can tell...." His voice trembled with uncertainty. But was he hesitant because he had not checked, or because the chain was moving but perhaps not "bouncing"?

"OK, call me back after you have taken a few more fixes. I'm going to keep heading towards town."

"Yes sir."

"Oh, and make sure Jenna does not sneak onto one of the water taxis and get ashore."

XO shot me a look, eyebrows raised, but did not say a word.

It was a risk to continue driving away from the ship, but I assessed that the *Vandy* was not dragging anchor. Even if it was, it would take a long time in those mild conditions to run aground. I showed confidence in J. R. and the crew...and I could still return in time if necessary.

J. R. called back in fifteen minutes.

"Captain, we took more fixes. The ship is *not dragging anchor*." His voice still had a little waver.

Although I maintained a calm countenance, my hand was sore when I unclenched it from the phone, and some inexplicable moisture had developed on my palms.

12.

KILLER TOMATO

Praise the Lord and pass the ammunition!

— Lieutenant (J. G.) Howell Maurice Forgy, chaplain,
during the Japanese attack on Pearl Harbor

The Sea of Japan was sunny and tranquil, a salty breeze cooling us. We had returned to our home waters and were operating alone off the coast. *Vandy* glided across smooth seas, no other ships in sight across the entire horizon. We were at sea for a week to exercise our engineering, damage control, operations, navigation, seamanship, and weapons teams. Of all those, shooting guns was our clear favorite. We had lots of them on board, from 9 mm handguns to a Gatling gun to our 76 mm main battery. Our guns were designed to target ships and aircraft, and their accuracy and dependability were critical to success in battle. We had other cool weapons too. Missiles and torpedoes, oh my! Lethal toys for boys.

And one furry girl.

Jenna had been aboard for months but was still acclimating to life on a ship. A crowded, bucking, oily-smelling metal ship. Although sure-footed, she was befuddled by the constant dynamic motion. She was meeting new people every day, a strain for a creature not too fond of human touch. At the same time, we were still getting used to having her aboard. So far the transition had gone well for everyone except the junior ensign, who had added Pee-way cleaning to his list of duties.

We were a bunch of grown-up boys when it came to guns and welcomed any chance to shoot ordnance. The crew was preparing to shoot the 76 mm Oto Melara gun, our main battery. This lethal weapon fired a twenty-seven-pound shell that sped at two thousand miles per hour to strike aircraft or ships. It was accurate and dependable, though shooting from a rocking ship meant our definition of "accurate" was different from what you achieve at the local gun range. And quick—it pumped out a shell a second! A shell that was ten times bigger than a standard rifle round and packed one hundred times more explosive punch than the largest bullet.

Vandy was in international waters, which meant that we could fire live ammunition. Everyone who was not on watch was topside to observe the gun shoot, one of the demonstrations that the entire crew could enjoy. Jenna was the guest of honor, trotting about the upper deck. She had shown a preference for being high in the ship where she could see and smell all that went past. This would be her first gun shoot, and I wondered how she would react. Jenna sensed the festive atmosphere of the assembled crew and went from one group to the next to ascertain what the party was about. Were there cookies?

The boatswain's mates inflated a ten-foot bright red cube, affectionately known as a "killer tomato," and pushed it to the railing. This target was a fleet favorite because it was easy to spot, compactly stored, inexpensive, and expendable. It was windy, so it took a few sailors to hold the giant cube in place until we were ready and then lift it over the lifelines. There was laughter as the enormous red cube tumbled from end to end across the tops of the waves, its large sail area catching the high winds. The gunner's mates faced a difficult shot today.

The first salvo was fired in rapid succession.

BOOM! BOOM! BOOM!

We all wore hearing protection and were braced for the sound percussion wave that struck us as we saw the blast of smoke exit the barrel.

All but one of us, that is.

Jenna leaped straight-legged from all four feet, using toe power to elevate, and yelped in panic, leaving a small puddle before sprinting to the ladder on the bridge. She was whimpering and shivering, about to attempt going down the treacherous ladder headfirst when I reached her. We halted the shoot, and I took our shell-shocked shipmate to the wardroom in the middle of the ship.

We searched for places to stash Jenna to mitigate her trauma and minimize her PTSD (Poor Traumatized Stressed Dog) during follow-on shoots. At first we tried the wardroom, her customary hangout located several decks below the gun. Matt LaPointe was chosen to watch her during the next gun shoot because he had just come off a five-hour watch and welcomed some Jenna therapy to relieve his tension. "Watching her" meant he was in the same room, on the same couch, watching a video.

He was absently petting Jenna, who was just within finger's reach, when the first round left the barrel. *Boom!* Jenna leaped into his lap, recreating a scene from *The Exorcist* by expelling everything she had out of every orifice. As the shots continued, Jenna shivered in fear. Matt, khaki uniform drenched in urine and splattered with liquid poop, called the bridge to report Jenna's "mishap."

We stopped the gunfire long enough to relocate Jenna deeper into the ship, down into the territory of the engineers. Although still scared, the engine noise and oily smells seemed to provide enough cover for her to survive with just a shiver or two.

We had not considered how loud explosions might affect Jenna and were determined not to repeat this oversight. We learned to put ourselves in Jenna's red coat before any new evolution. I would like to report that Jenna became desensitized to the gun, acclimated to its sound and fury. But she never did. In fact, without fail she started shivering days ahead of a gun shoot. We endeavored for a year to determine what precursors she could see or smell, a topic of debate at both the wardroom and chief's mess tables. We did not start any pre-shoot processes more than twenty-four hours ahead of time. Moreover, the activity related to the gun was done far from where Jenna lived or travelled. Perhaps she smelled the powder or heard something unique, but we never figured it out.

We developed a pre-gun shoot checklist for Jenna that included a doggy tranquilizer prescribed by the Army veterinarian, cotton balls in her ears, and placing her down in main control with the engineers. All we could do was comfort her, and on the day of a shoot take her into the depths of the ship where she was far from the gun and surrounded by continuous machine noises and sweaty, doting engineers. This system helped, but she suffered from PTSD for the rest of her life. A loud noise, such as a balloon popping, would startle her and bring shivers for ten minutes until she was certain there were no more "shots" coming. After Jenna retired, I spent every Fourth of July sitting with her in an interior bathroom of my house, radio blasting, cotton balls installed and treats at hand.

Although Jenna hated the big gun the most, she did not appreciate any of our weapons. Each made loud sounds and strange odors that assaulted her finer senses. Another offender was R2-D2. The white dome-shaped figure looked out over the flight deck, commanding a three-hundred-degree view from the highest deck. Rather than blinking lights and beeps, our version of R2-D2 sported a multi-barreled machine gun protruding from his abdomen. His given name was CIWS (pronounced "sea-wiz," it stands for close-in weapon system), and he was our last line of defense against missiles, aircraft, and even small surface craft. This Phalanx Gatling cannon fired 1,500 20 mm rounds in twenty seconds. Try to imagine that. Seventy-five large bullets every second, the definition of a "hail of bullets." R2-D2 would shiver as he tracked and centered on a target, then shoot bullets at 2,400 mph with a short, metallic *BRRRRRRAAACCCK* (to replicate the sound, press your lips together, bottom lip overlapping the top, and forcefully push air out for five seconds) followed by a large puff of smoke and scores of ejected casings. Jenna could hear, or feel, R2-D2 from anywhere in the ship. Her head would lower, ears retract, and she would start panting. At least with R2-D2, it was over quickly.

Missiles were our longest-range weapons. SM-1 missiles targeted enemy aircraft and missiles within twenty miles. These fifteen-foot missiles hit Mach 2 to intercept and destroy air threats with 137 pounds of high explosives. The MK-13 missile launcher, nicknamed the "One-Armed Bandit" because it held one missile at a time, was located on the bow of the ship. The magazine below the launcher held forty missiles. We could also launch Harpoon cruise missiles to attack ships and surfaced submarines. These missiles skimmed just above the sea at five hundred knots for up to sixty-five miles, making them difficult to detect and counter. We did not launch any missiles while Jenna was on board.

Vandy also had weapons for targets under the sea. We had a three-tube torpedo launcher on each side of the ship. Our five-hundred-pound MK-46 torpedoes traveled at forty knots for up to six miles. This was not our favorite weapon. We were at a disadvantage against submarines, which could usually detect the ship well before we found them. So getting within six miles of a submarine, and its superior torpedoes, was not our best option. At least the torpedo launches were quiet and quick, which was important since they occurred near Jenna's beloved smoke deck.

One of the most important parts of the *Vandy* warfighting team was the helicopter detachment (HSL Det). We embarked two SH-60B Seahawk helicopters whenever we got underway for an extended time. It was critical to meld the Det with the rest of the crew quickly, for the helos (helicopters) were the wide receivers on our team, extending the field and putting the opponent at risk. Having a helo swung the advantage to us in many scenarios, especially when conducting anti-submarine or anti-ship operations. Our Seahawk could push out to one hundred miles, drop a field of sonobuoys to detect a submarine, then drop a MK-46 torpedo on his unsuspecting ass. This was how we got that sole kill during RIMPAC. Even if they did not damage the sub, at least they put it on the defensive and made it maneuver at high speed, creating noise we could detect.

Jenna decided over time that she liked the embarked aviators. She spent time with them in the wardroom, shared their bunks, and enjoyed their pool. More on the pool later. She got special treatment, even spending time in the helos. It would have broken safety rules—and might well have scared her—to fly with them, so she never got airborne. As far as I know....

The sea can be soothing and peaceful, or violent and perilous. We loved placid days but had to grit it out when it was tempestuous. We wouldn't get to choose the weather when we fought the ship, so we prepared for all conditions. One time was almost fatal.

We were participating in Foal Eagle, a two-week exercise to improve our warfighting teamwork with the South Korean Navy and to flex our muscles in North Korea's front yard. This may have been an exercise, but the two Korean navies were not shy about exchanging gunfire if they found themselves in the same patch of ocean. Winter had arrived early off the Korean Peninsula; it was a completely different environment from our killer tomato shoot of just a month ago. We were a late add to the exercise, replacing a ship with engineering trouble. *Vandy*'s engineers had the ship purring, and the combat systems guys had our weapons systems primed.

We were so pumped that we added ourselves to a naval gunfire support (NGFS) exercise. NGFS is when ships fire their guns to take out enemy positions in support of Marines taking the beach. It was not a mission for our class of ship, as our gun was not designed for that mission. But we wanted to try, so the gunner's mates found a way to shoot our 76 mm gun against targets set up on an offshore island. Unsure if a frigate had ever done this, we planned meticulously to ensure we had it right. That meticulous planning included determining who had tactical control (TACON) of Jenna for this event, and what her noise-mitigation protocol would be. Game day arrived, and we rolled in at twenty knots firing like a gunslinger. Hit after hit, *Vandy* outscored most of the other ships. More proof that sailors, not systems, were the most important part of any equation.

We also tracked submarine targets, the sonar technicians finding them despite turbulent wintry conditions. We even got to shoot two exercise torpedoes. Shooting them was fun...but recovering them was not. The skies were leaden gray, spitting frozen rain that dashed sideways in the high winds. Whitecaps lined the tops of ten-foot waves, the wind whipping the tops into a freezing, salty spray. The sultry embrace of Hawaii was a world away. Jenna took shelter inside the bridge, curling up in a corner. Even her curiosity was frozen by these conditions. We put over a boat to recover our torpedoes that were bobbing on gray, churning seas.

We used the ship's bulk to provide a lee (shelter) from winds and seas while launching the boat, but it was still dangerous. These seas caused the ship to roll from side to side, and as soon as the twenty-six-foot boat touched the water, it bucked and kicked like a bull. The boat crew frantically released themselves from the davit hook, and Boatswain's Mate Tom Hengel motored away from the swaying ship. Winds howled at twenty-five knots, blowing frozen rain horizontally across the bleak seascape. We guided the boat to the first torpedo, and the swimmer jumped into the frigid sea to attach a line. They recovered the swimmer and towed the torpedo back to the ship, where we hauled it aboard. It took almost an hour to find and retrieve the second torpedo, as it had drifted and was difficult to spot in those rollers. We recovered the crew after two hours of frozen hell, and I assembled them on the mess decks so the corpsman and I could judge their condition. Frozen smiles on each face, they resembled tall Smurfs.

"That was some shit out there. How are you guys?"

"Ca-ca-ca-ca-captain, th-th-thaat was w-w-wiild!" stammered Tom. He had a semi-crazed look about him, Jack Nicholson with Smurf-blue skin. He swayed as if still on the small boat.

The rescue swimmer stripped out of his dry suit and tried to restore blood flow to his skin by vigorously scouring it with a towel. He smiled through clenched teeth, unable to unclench them to speak. Jenna moved over to him, sniffing curiously and staring at his face.

She sat, lowered her head, and whimpered while holding my eyes with hers.

I had never heard anything like this from her or seen this behavior. I took a closer look. These sailors were on the edge of hypothermia, despite their brave faces. I instructed the corpsman to check them thoroughly and keep them under observation.

"You guys deserve a medal, but I have something better. Doc, give each man a shot."

Heads snapped up, quizzical smiles turning to grins as they realized that I did not mean a shot with a needle.

I broke out a bottle of ceremonial soju given to me by our Korean hosts, firewater that burns the throat and ignites a bonfire inside. This was the only time that I ever authorized alcohol consumption at sea.

That shot did the trick.

I'm not sure if it was the alcohol or the fact that they were allowed a drink at sea that provided the bigger kick. But I do know that Jenna's perception saved four sailors from a serious situation, perhaps even death. She remained with the boat crew and corpsman until they were fully recovered, maintaining her own *dog watch*.

13.

RED BULL SHARK

A ship is referred to as she
because it costs so much to keep
one in paint and powder.

— FLEET ADMIRAL CHESTER NIMITZ

Navy ship is a small town, without the football field. Every service that is provided to an apartment complex must also be provided to sailors at sea, except we are also the service providers. A ship provides its own electricity, plumbing, sewage and waste treatment, heating and air conditioning, compressed air, welding and parts fabrication, gas turbine/engine/motor/generator service and repair, small boat upkeep, hull and deck upkeep and painting, fuel and oil maintenance, medical diagnosis and emergency triage, air rescue flights, laundry and pressing services, parts inventory and global support, barber, voice and satellite communications, electrical and electronics repair, budgeting/payroll/ATM, navigation, global mail delivery, interior cleaning/shampooing/painting, law enforcement/security, and entertainment.

On *Vandy*, we added doggie day care, grooming, and walking. And specialized medical diagnosis by Nurse Jenna.

The basics to support life—water, food, and oxygen—were not so easily obtained at sea. We were far from cables and pipes and couldn't go to the local water authority or grocery store. Our groceries were resupplied by vertical replenishment (VERTREP), which was helicopters dropping five-hundred-pound pallets on our flight deck, with the crew racing to clear and stow them between flights. Imagine Amazon delivering a year's worth of stuff to your driveway in a thirty-minute span. Food was stored in big freezers and storage areas, and when those were full, the rest was stuffed into exhaust fan rooms, out-of-the-way passageways, and other nooks.

The culinary specialists prepared every meal on board. Junior sailors rotated as mess cooks to scour pots and pans, clean the galley and mess decks, and pick up the spaces. Despite their name, their work was all mess and no cooking. Sailors who envisaged themselves firing missiles and navigating ships instead started their careers slogging through menial duties like those done in a fast-food establishment by teenagers.

At meal time I would spot the top of a red-and-cream tail cruising between the blue plastic mess deck tables, a red bull shark hunting for food that had fallen overboard from someone's plate. Jenna did not lie down during meals, always cruising, ready to pounce. She watched for telltale signs, knowing that the best chance of spillage was when someone stood up from the table. As soon as a sailor finished eating, she was on alert, moving next to his chair to stare at his plastic plate. She was not driven by hunger—she got plenty of wholesome dog food. I believed her ravenous attitude was from her time on the streets, an ingrained habit to gobble down as much as she could whenever she had the chance.

Food was important, but water was our most critical resource. We could store only a limited amount of water, so the engineers had to transform seawater into potable water. Although today's reverse-osmosis systems make this simple, on *Vandy* we used steam to remove impurities. This tedious and fragile method often resulted in water shortfalls, which triggered hated "water hours." That meant showers were prohibited when reserves ran low in order to preserve water for vital requirements.

Even the air we breathed could not be taken for granted. We provided ventilation throughout the ship, especially to those hot, murky machinery spaces buried deep in the bowels. Our Gas Free Engineer tested spaces that were typically sealed to ensure they were safe to enter. And we had to be able to provide nontoxic air throughout the ship in the event of a chemical or biological gas attack.

When in port—about two-thirds of the time—the work did not stop, it just changed. Most of that time was spent preparing the ship and crew to operate at sea. The engineers, nicknamed "snipes," were the hardest-working tribe on any ship. They maintained and repaired every engine, gas turbine, generator, boat engine, and anything else that used fuel. The engineer was equal to any rocket scientist, except he worked in a lab that was hot/humid/dim/cramped/rolling and was held to an impossible timeline. He often had to improvise when missing proper tools or parts, for which he could get in trouble. But he needed to get the job done *now*. The snipes kept the entire ship running, yet their pay was on par with that of a fresh-faced manager of a fast-food joint.

A ship is like a huge and complex car from an engineering standpoint. *Vandy* was propelled by two massive gas turbine engines, the same type used to power jumbo jets. Each gas turbine delivered forty-one thousand shaft horsepower, two hundred times more than your car. Combine this power with our controllable-pitch propeller, which allowed us to apply that power immediately in any direction without having to reverse the direction the shaft was turning, and we had a maritime drag racer.

And we did race.

Every once in a while, when a few ships congregated, we drag raced. Lined up five hundred yards apart, the ships bobbed while engineers primped their plants to get the most out of them. Pride and bragging rights were at stake. One ship blew its whistle, and we were off.

NEAL J. KUSUMOTO, CAPTAIN, US NAVY (RET)

Accelerating across the water, we watched to see who had the fastest start. Jenna felt the excitement of the crew, not knowing why there was a happy tension in the air but wanting to partake. The crew lined the rails and cheered as we surged ahead of our competitors. Jenna pranced behind the throng, pushing her head between legs to get a view of the race and looking up at faces trying to determine what was so fascinating.

Vandy jumped ahead and held the lead for the first mile, but shoulders slumped as we inevitably lost ground. The bigger cruisers and destroyers eventually passed us, brute horsepower making up for lesser proficiency. This was one of the few times the engineers were the focus of something fun, when their skill and hard work were highlighted by the unrivaled performance of the plant. After the race I watched as sailors knelt to pet Jenna, caressing her head or trailing their fingers along her back. She sat motionless, regally blasé.

This race was more than just a playful diversion or chest-thumping test of power. Speed and maneuverability are keys to fighting at sea, enabling us to optimize the range of sensors and weapons. Imagine swarms of patrol boats speeding toward the ship at forty knots, each carrying missiles similar to the ones that disabled the frigate USS *Stark* in 1987 during the Iran-Iraq War. We wouldn't have enough time to destroy all those boats before they got within range to launch their weapons, and it would only take one chance hit to disable us. But the sea is rarely perfectly calm, and a frigate can make better speed than smaller craft when there are waves. That switches the advantage back to us, where our better stability and longer-range weapons would prevail.

Our ability to maneuver and employ speed saved the ship from a cataclysmic collision in Hong Kong harbor. The fog was a heavy, dripping blanket that kept the crew straining to see beyond our lifelines as we entered the channel. Ship horns wailed all around us in this teeming waterway, dampened and distorted by the sodden fog. We couldn't determine which direction they were emanating from, or how far away the vessels were. Jenna was underfoot, pacing and whining, adding to our unease. A quartermaster scooped her up and took her into the chart room, easing her stress and ours. We spotted a ship on radar that was on a collision course with us. We were in a narrow channel with no room to maneuver without putting ourselves into a head-on situation with outgoing ships. We had the right of way, which meant we were required to maintain course and speed.

I slowed anyway. This provided additional time to deal with the threat ahead of us but increased our susceptibility to being rammed from behind.

We called the ghost ship repeatedly on the emergency channel.

Dead silence. The distance was one thousand yards and closing fast.

We sounded low-visibility fog signals, loud resonating blasts that could be heard for many miles.

Nothing.

Five hundred yards and still on a collision course. And we still could not see him.

We sounded six short blasts as a last resort, the danger signal to any mariner! Jenna leaped to her feet, eyes wide and tail between her legs. She ran from the chart room, looking up at our faces to determine the meaning of these earsplitting blasts. We had no time to comfort her.

Not a sound from the merchant, and our radar showed that he was not maneuvering or changing speed. We backed down hard, screws digging into the water, taking our headway off quickly. A worn freighter materialized, trailing ethereal fog tendrils as it cut across our bow, so close we could see two people in its pilot house. We watched, entranced and angry, as the darkened ship passed silently a mere fifty yards ahead. It vanished into the fog without any sign that its crew even knew we were there.

The pilot explained, after I was done cussing, that it was a Chinese custom to maneuver close to another ship to "rub off" bad spirits before entering port. I was just glad we hadn't rubbed off any paint; even a minor collision could have cost millions and taken our warship offline for months. I ordered "ahead full" to get back up to speed quickly, knowing there were ships coming up behind us. Being at a standstill was like your car stalling in the middle lane of the interstate in heavy fog.

This close call was a precursor to a much more dangerous, and premeditated, threat that we would confront in Hong Kong.

14.

CHIEFS AND BLUEJACKETS

Everything I ever learned about leadership,
I learned from a Chief Petty Officer.

— Senator John McCain

On the fifth day God created the sailor. And it was good, and wicked, and lots of rollicking fun. Which led to sea stories, tasteless tattoos, and an arrest or two....

When God started work on the sailor, he[2] was a bit tired from creating the world and mankind and such. It was Friday afternoon at about 1700 (5:00 p.m.), and he knew that Saturday was his duty day before he got that seventh day to rest.

But there was one more thing that he had to do.

He might have indulged in a sip or two of *spirits* to relax and get his creative juices flowing. Ready for some liberty of his own, he scanned his ethereal workshop for the proper materials to complete his final task after a long day of creating.

It was time to craft a *sailor*.

To form the sailor's backbone, he chose steel, the same material used for the keel of Navy ships, strong yet flexible, ready to stand up to the toughest challenges. He then dipped his hand seven times, each time into a different sea,[3] and filled the heart and veins. God then reached deep into the Pacific and scooped magma from undersea volcanoes, putting fire into the sailor's belly and loins. Finally, he melded ingredients from his favorite animals. The sailor was fashioned to be crafty like the raven, as brave as the wolf, as tenacious as the badger, as adaptable and unruly as the coyote, as smart as the dolphin, as regal as an eagle, and an alpha predator like the orca. And as self-sufficient as a Shiba Inu.

God stepped back to scrutinize his newest creation. Strong in body, mind, and opinion. Ready to fight, ready to fu...love.

He was content.

A ship is only as good as the sailors that make up its crew. Sailors are much more important than R2-D2 or even the sewage treatment system. Without trained and motivated sailors, nothing works well. A ship's company is broken into three parts: the Wardroom (officers), Chief's Mess, and bluejackets. Enlisted sailors are broken into nine rates that denote seniority, from the clueless seaman recruit (E-1) to the salty master chief (E-9). E-1 through E-3 are the apprentices, new guys who do all the dirty jobs. E-4 through E-6 are the petty officers, the first line of leadership and management. E-7 is a chief, E-8 a senior chief, and E-9 a revered master chief. Each sailor also has a rating, or specialty, such as electrician, sonar technician, or quartermaster. There were twenty-four ratings on *Vandy*. By combining rate and rating, one knew exactly where a person fit. Jenna never advanced beyond seaman despite handling multiple duties that included culinary specialist, crew morale manager, medical prognosticator, food lookout, and napping professional.

It's not where you come from but where you're heading that matters in the Navy. Most sailors join the Navy to get ahead in life. Every sailor has a chance to lead and manage, to take responsibility and be held accountable, to be relevant to the success or failure of the ship. Each can see that with hard work and dedication she will soon advance; there is no ceiling. Sailors advance every two to three years early in their careers. As they become more senior, the timeline is dependent on their performance, professional knowledge, and time in grade. Their chance of putting on khakis and joining the Chief's Mess is around 20 percent, and only the very best advance to senior and master chief.

What about the officers? If still breathing after eleven years, there is a good chance of being promoted to lieutenant commander. After that the going gets tough, with only a few selected for higher ranks and command. Jenna rose from recruit to the upper ranks at seven times the normal rate, which corresponded with her faster aging process. But no matter how high her rank rose, she retained her name as Seaman Jenna as a tribute to the sailors who did the grueling work on the ship.

Sailors spend much of their career at sea, apart from family and the niceties of living in a house that most people take for granted. The Navy mans the fleet using a policy called the sea/shore rotation. A sailor can expect to spend four to six years at sea followed by a three-year shore tour, then repeat the cycle. Jenna, always the exception, spent her entire "career" at sea. No wonder she took off for a few hours ashore from time to time.

As sailors get more senior, they spend more time ashore as administrators and instructors to prepare the next generation. Senior Chief Skip Triplett, my senior engineer, had a typical career. *Vandy* was his third ship, and at that point he had deployed away from home for six years. When you added all the time he was at sea, he had been separated from his family for 60 percent of his career. All that time away was spent deep in the ships' spaces fixing engines and keeping the plant going. You might believe he was well compensated, perhaps like someone on an oil rig. Not so, he made around $3,000 a month.

In 1999 a seaman recruit made $850 a month, a chief with ten years' service made $2,100, and a master chief with twenty-five years made $3,500. A shiny new ensign made $1,800, a mid-grade lieutenant $3,300, and

I as a commander made $4,700. When deployed from home for more than twenty-nine consecutive days, we received an additional $100 a month to compensate for being separated from our family. That did not fill the family coffers or pay for the kids' college education, but it did cover one or two phone calls from some foreign port (reminder: this was before cell phones or the internet).

The working class of a ship is comprised of sailors who enlisted. These sailors are called "bluejackets," a term dating back to when British sailors wore short blue coats. They do the grueling work, fight the fires, and drive the ship. Like the Chief's Mess and Wardroom, I was blessed with an incredible group who succeeded throughout long careers. Many became officers and chiefs. Seaman Jenna was in this pack, though more of a "redjacket." This was where all good sailors started, and she, too, had to prove herself.

The chief's mess is the beating heart of every Navy ship. The "mess" can mean either the space where they eat or the group of chiefs, similar to the use of the word "wardroom." It was the chiefs' dining establishment, meeting place, sanctuary, and lounge. If they were not working or sleeping, they could be found in the mess. Chief Petty Officers had risen through the ranks to become middle management and had proven, through hard work, dedication, and intelligence, that they were both experts in their field and good leaders. Some had college degrees, but they all earned their khaki uniforms and combination covers through blood, sweat, and beers. The chiefs are a strong entity on every ship, the leaders on the deck plates who make the organization run smoothly and effectively. They have the most experience and are experts in their fields, and without them any ship would founder. After three command tours and many years at sea, I knew that the Chief's Mess was the most critical group. When the chiefs are empowered to be leaders on the deck plates, the ship is sure to succeed.

The *Vandy* Chief's Mess was the strongest I had ever seen. You were either with this incredible band of twenty old salts or needed to move out of their way. In fact, eleven of them became commissioned officers, and Tony Fortson went on to command a destroyer, which is about as rare as winning the lottery. These salty seamen had been in for ten to twenty-three years, most of it at sea, and had already tried any good idea twice. They had settled into their own routine, which revolved around the mess.

No one just barged into the mess. Even as the captain I knocked before entering and seldom bothered them. The only non-chief who had a pass to enter and leave at will was Jenna. Despite her seaman status, she frequently sauntered in. And perhaps got a bite of donut. I did get invited for coffee, entering past a row of cups hanging from the bulkhead, one for each chief. These cups were all sizes and shapes but had one thing in common: they were crusty with stains from years of harsh shipboard coffee, each brown strata a testament to that chief's time in the Navy. I once heard of some poor mess cook, thinking he was going above and beyond the call, who washed all the chiefs' coffee cups. His proud presentation of clean tableware was met by incredulous gasps... and his life became hell. Even I dared not suggest that the chiefs clean these ancient relics that contained their individual histories, like the rings of a tree.

One day the chief's mess was thrown into chaos.

Chief Barnacle (name changed to protect the scarred) had developed an infection. After many appointments, they determined the cause and effect. The cause of the chief's infection was traced to his coffee cup, encrusted not only with old coffee but also with a batch of germs. The effect was that he had a testicle cut out.

Every man just crossed his legs, cringed, and gritted his teeth.

Our balls are our center mass. They are central to sex, a driving force for males, and our biggest vulnerability. Ladies can manipulate men by manipulating these orbs, or drop them to their knees with a well-aimed kick. Men protect their family jewels with cups and jockstraps, and yet refuse to wear a helmet while speeding on a motorcycle.

I visited the mess later that week, taking Jenna with me to have coffee with the new master chief, Craig Morey. She stood stock still as I gathered her into my arms for the climb down several sets of ladders, then huffed when I set her down. She looked up at my face, trying to decipher what was next. I stuck my tongue out at her. Her face remained inscrutable, eyes dark and unblinking.

"Let's go to the chief's mess!"

Jenna blinked once, and her lips turned up slightly into what seemed to be a smile. She turned and led the way to the Home of Donuts, not bothering to look back to see if I was keeping up. She waited for me at the door, and after knocking we entered. I grinned in wonder at the gleaming coffee cups hanging from the wall. Craig shrugged, then a big smile broke out and we both chuckled.

Sailors have a love-hate relationship with the Navy, despite that we all volunteered. You have already been introduced to the phrase "I love the fuckin' Navy...and the Navy loves fuckin' me." This is said when something unpleasant is at hand, usually with a sardonic smile and a that's-the-way-it-goes attitude. It exemplifies the complicated familial relationship in which the Navy acts as a slightly-out-of-touch parent and the sailor as a misunderstood teen.

Most sailors do in fact love the fuckin' Navy, because we believe in what it stands for and can put up with the bureaucratic bumbling that comes with any large organization. It is rarely personal. Orders to an unwelcome job or location, an accelerated deployment that forces us from home and family earlier than expected, weekend duty, reduced promotion opportunities. All are understandable, though not appreciated. The needs of the Navy come before the needs of individuals. We understand this and are willing to risk our lives in battle to protect hearth and home.

A sailor is as wise as any philosopher; think of Aristotle with a porn habit. He can think deep thoughts but prefers simple, direct ones. Sailors are uncannily smart; they can see through any trite "good news" for what it is. Their beer goggles have a BS lens that filters anything less than unvarnished truth. Bad news won't be applauded, but it will be respected as truth. This coping mechanism is well developed because sailors put up with a lot of rancid news. Deployments away from home that are extended for months, the timeline to start another deployment accelerated, port calls cancelled, meat labeled "Deliver only to military and penitentiaries," loves and families lost.

After we returned to port from one training period, I disembarked then remembered that I had forgotten something. I returned to the ship and signaled the watch team not to bong me aboard and disturb everyone. As I climbed up to the deserted second deck, I heard sniffling from a door that was ajar. I approached quietly, intrigued by this rare emotional display. I listened as a young man wondered how his wife could leave him. He explained that he had tried to be a better husband, but nothing worked. Things just got worse, and now she wasn't even here to greet him when the ship returned to port. Hearing no reply, I peeked around the door. Jenna was lying down, head between her paws, eyes looking up at him.

It wasn't uncommon for a sailor to return home from sea to find...nothing...his wife or girlfriend having moved on with his children, car, dog, TV, and the rest of their stuff. It was as if he were living the lyrics of a country song.

I slipped away, leaving Jenna to wield her unsought power of therapy. I tipped off the Master Chief before I left about this young sailor's heartache. The sacrifices of being in the Navy, of being away from home for half a year, often stretched relationships past their breaking point. We couldn't repair marriages, but we did ensure shipmates didn't go through these travails alone.

Not all heroes are covered in blood or medals.

Most sailors do not have to surrender their lives, but they do give up their daily privileges and rights in order to keep the world safe. To make it a better place. Although sailors are willing to go into combat and fight to their last breath, their sacrifice is usually over the long haul. Months and years at sea away from home and family, without the same right to free speech or legal representation, and paid near the poverty level. They do not offer their lives in order to attain eternal glory, but because they are patriots ready to die without our knowledge or thanks.

15.

THE SHERIFF'S BADGE

A true leader has the confidence to stand alone,
the courage to make tough decisions,
and the compassion to listen
to the needs of others.

— GENERAL DOUGLAS MACARTHUR

The US Navy is showing the American flag around the world as you read this. As it has been doing for more than seventy years. The fleet is demonstrating that it is ready and willing to use force in order to maintain peace. Many view the Navy as the world's policeman, usually meant as a compliment but a poor analogy. We are peacekeepers, a deterrent to those who would take advantage of the weak.

To meet these lofty goals, Navy ships must perform numerous critical missions to near perfection: to defend the aircraft carrier, to defend the US or other countries from ballistic missiles that could have nuclear warheads, to seek out and destroy enemy submarines and ships, to escort merchants, and to fight pirates. Failure in battle means death and destruction.

A Navy ship captain is truly *the man*. It seems a bit much as I sit writing in a sterile room, an archaic function left over from the days of sail and floggings. But military structure is based upon our unique role as warfighters, and every member must respond immediately to commands. Today's warfare is fought in minutes; decisions must be made and executed quickly. Seconds matter, with life or death in the balance. Inbound missiles or aircraft approaching at many times the speed of sound don't allow for questions or discussion, or for equipment not primed and ready.

The sheer power of command at sea is incomparable. Command is an elixir, equal parts intoxicating authority and stifling responsibility. Every member of the crew, officers and enlisted, looked to me to make perfect decisions. Instantly.

Where to navigate the ship, what speed, what engineering setup, what combat systems to employ and when to engage the enemy, who could re-enlist, how many people had to stay onboard every night—the list was endless, decisions required night and day. While officers and chiefs made many decisions, I always made the final call for critical matters.

Life-or-death responsibility created intense stress. While I talked with the XO and CMC about all things related to the ship, I could not shift any of the weight from my own shoulders. I was accountable for the entire ship and crew, for everything that we did. The sole being that I could talk to about my private thoughts and fears was a taciturn, indifferent young sailor.

Seaman Jenna.

I would sit on *her* couch when I was tense. Her head would slowly rise, and after looking at my hands (*no cookies?*), her eyes would lift to meet mine. Then she'd lay her head back between her paws, dark eyes continuing to watch me as I stroked her back and laid out whatever was troubling me. Her eyes closed, her breathing slowed. I continued lightly petting Jenna while I talked, her relaxed body warm against my hand. My eyes stayed open, but my breathing and heart rate decelerated. My shoulders relaxed; only then did I realize that I had been pushing them up toward my ears. The tension in my frame ebbed, the tide of my stress flowing out of me.

Jenna never seemed concerned about the issues that I brought up, always letting me do the talking. In fact, at times I heard what sounded like a light snore. Like any good psychoanalyst, she let me talk my way through the dilemma. But her patience did have limits. If I overstayed my welcome on her couch, she blinked one eye open and loudly sighed through her nose.

Being the captain is like being a rock star interspersed with periods of being Darth Vader, except without the costumes, surrounded by people who depend on you to keep them out of the water...and having a good time while doing it. When I walked into any space or room, the sailors sounded off, "Attention on deck!"

and snapped to rigid attention until I put them at ease. Stopping to look at a piece of equipment in the passageway, for even a minute, could lead the crew to spend hours trying to determine what had caught my eye, what was wrong, and how to make it right before I walked by again. Perhaps it was a moment of reflection, or a minor interest in some small item. I had to remember that my every action could lead to unanticipated work, even if that was not my intent. I had to remain aware of this power and apply it judiciously.

When I left the ship I was rarely alone. The captain is, by definition, popular. Not necessarily liked, but on center stage. The clear and rapt attention received from the crew turned heads in public, which could boost the ego. It could also be trouble. An entourage brings instant attention, everyone drawn to the power of celebrity. We teach those going to command that putting on the star-shaped pin designating command at sea, called a "sheriff's badge," does not make anyone better looking or funnier...it just seems that way.

Power attracts people and sometimes leads naval officers, in their mid-life and prone to heavy drinking, down paths they regret. Binge drinking, driving under the influence, adultery, or other poor decisions lead to the demise of some. An officer who licks the grains of popularity from the V of his thumb and forefinger and then rockets a shot of liquid courage into his gullet will often taste bitterness far beyond that of a lemon. Power mixed with alcohol can be a heady—and deadly—mix.

I know, because I would fall into this trap on my next ship. But that is another story.

The captain must be an officer and a gentleman, a warrior who stands above others in tactical prowess and personal behavior. The father of the US Navy, John Paul Jones, said it best:

> "It is by no means enough that an officer of the Navy should be a capable mariner.... He should be as well a gentleman of liberal education, refined manners, punctilious courtesy, and the nicest sense of personal honor."

Being in command has been compared to being a king, and it still retains some royal features. In what other job does someone control the fate of those who work for him? More than just fate, one is entrusted with their future. The Navy is composed predominantly of young adults between seventeen and twenty-two years old; when they report to their first ship, they are still maturing, still figuring out their identity, priorities, and values. Most will not make the naval service a career but will spend four or six years serving. They come from wildly diverse backgrounds. Some are from broken homes or underprivileged neighborhoods, some got off on the wrong foot at a young age, some are from wealthy backgrounds, and some are from Main Street USA.

One even came from a dog shelter.

It was my job to help young sailors complete the growing-up process, to fire the clay their parents had molded. On board, they learned accountability for their actions and for the actions of their shipmates. They learned to be responsible for jobs affecting the readiness of the entire ship. They learned commitment to an institution, to their ship, and to their shipmates. They could not just walk away when things didn't go their way.

I sat down to chat with every member of my crew in what became known as "Coffee with the captain." I wanted to hear their goals and dreams, to find out about their family and home, to listen to them. This was not a bitch session or open invitation to criticize their chain of command, or even a counseling session, but rather time to get to know one another. Sometimes embarrassing problems were discussed, or someone presented a good idea they had been afraid to share. We rarely drank coffee; the sailor was usually too nervous.

Seated on the small couch across from me, each was nervous to be in the captain's cabin. Not that my 150 pounds was physically imposing, but being alone with the captain was a first for most of them. However, I had a magic red icebreaker.

Seaman Jenna.

She would leisurely greet each sailor, sniffing the visitor while allowing him to pet her. He'd visibly relax, calmed by a compatriot who often hung out with the crew. She would stroll over to *her* couch and lie down, rolling out her tongue like a red carpet as she yawned. Her routine always brought a smile to our guest. Her relaxed mood eased the rigid sailor, whose posture would soften. He might even sit back against his seat.

I was careful with how I dealt with any ship-related issues brought up in this forum, waiting a few weeks before addressing the issue so it would not be related to those private meetings. After hundreds of sessions, I knew my sailors and got a broad view of what young people were looking for when they joined the Navy.

Join the Navy, See the World! Although a dated advertisement, many still join to see the world. Sailors enlist for three other reasons: to get an education, to get away from a bad situation or to break out of a limited future, and to serve their country. Young people often get to fulfill all four...and get much more than they expected. Two of these reasons are intrinsically about bettering themselves to improve their situation and station in life. One reason is about service to a higher calling, while seeing the world is purely about fun.

Sailors leave the Navy with a sense of honor, a clear understanding of accountability, an ability to follow through on assignments, and leadership and management experience. They also have a broader perspective of the world, having now experienced it, and as a result open their minds beyond the physical and mental boundaries of their old neighborhoods.

The Navy is well worth your tax dollars. Sailors are working hard at sea right now to keep you safe, and have pledged their lives to protect your way of life. Their families are enduring their own hardships, alone and living on marginal funds, all without fanfare or thanks. At the same time, the Navy is crafting good citizens who return to civilian life as stable, hardworking men and women. Veterans are proud, upstanding members of the community who lead church fundraisers and organize golf tournaments for worthy causes. They will not be tenuous or fearful, but forthright and forthcoming. Each has already worked hard, persevered in stressful situations, been separated from family and home for long periods, and thrived in challenging, unpredictable situations. They will become leaders in their communities who stand for what is right. They have seen the other side of the world and understand all that America stands for, appreciating both our bounty and our role as the leader of the free world.

There is no better job than commanding a warship; it is the pinnacle of our naval profession. One may go on to higher postings, but they will have neither the importance nor personal satisfaction of being *the captain*. Command of a ship, or a submarine, or a squadron of aircraft...what it comes down to is leading a talented, diverse, motivated, energetic, and patriotic group of young Americans.

16.

KEEPING THE CAT IN THE BAG

'Tis skill, not strength, that governs a ship.

— THOMAS FULLER

Did I say Darth Vader?

The captain of a ship has judicial powers far wider than those of any judge. His decisions are unassailable. I have seen a body hanging from the mast of another country's naval ship, which was definitely unassailable. Although hanging is no longer an option in our Navy, a court martial can order capital punishment for a case referred from a ship. In days of yore the punishment for most serious crimes was flogging, administered by the bosun's mate using a whip called a cat o' nine tails. The "cat" was kept in a red-dyed bag, and it was a sorry sailor who faced a *cat let out of the bag*.

A Commanding Officer no longer has anyone flogged but does have many other options. I could have put someone into a Marine Corps brig to exist on bread and water for three days. Three days under Marine guidance while on this special diet gained the attention of even the hardest case. I could have taken away half of someone's pay for two months and restricted them to the ship, even discharged him from the Navy. All this, and more, is within the purview of the Commanding Officer. Usually, I just had to get the sailor's attention, get him back on track.

The Uniform Code of Military Justice (UCMJ) defines military law, granting the Commanding Officer wide latitude to pass judgment and mete out punishment. The UCMJ is based upon the unique military situation where acts of individuals could result in many deaths. In a battle there is no time to consult lawyers. The word of the Commanding Officer must be sacrosanct, or orders might be questioned at a precarious moment.

The "court" on a ship where a "trial" is held is called captain's mast. Before it gets to that stage, the entire chain of command has reviewed the case. First, a chief or officer promptly conducted a thorough investigation. The chiefs then interviewed the accused sailor, his chain of command, and witnesses before recommending either holding mast or dismissing the case. The XO then carried out his own inquiry, in a smaller forum held in his stateroom, and provided his recommendations. I then received a folder with the sailor's record, the results of the investigation, and pre-mast hearing recommendations. All this happened in a few days; we didn't want it simmering longer than necessary.

I hated captain's mast, viewing it as a last resort. There was no burden of proof when someone went to captain's mast. I looked at what information we had, got a quick statement from witnesses and the accused's chain of command and then made a decision. It went into effect immediately. Grown men cried, understanding too late the consequences of their actions. I ended careers and changed lives, but I didn't do it casually. Every sailor got a fair chance, though not all got a second chance.

Rarely was there a question of guilt or anyone pleading innocent. The primary difficulty was assessing the implications of the act and its impact on the ship and crew. Drug use was an automatic out; I discharged good sailors because of one bad decision made late at night. Fighting, especially on board, was dealt with severely as it broke apart the team and showed a lack of judgment and restraint. Theft was not tolerated. We lived together in a confined space and couldn't have someone we didn't trust living in our house. Sleeping on watch was one of the most heinous transgressions, putting the ship and everyone's lives in jeopardy.

The penalty had to fit the crime, the individual, the crew, and the family. It had to be consistent with previous penalties for similar transgressions. The accused might not have as many rights as civilians but did receive special treatment. I knew him, his situation, his background and upward mobility, his family and their needs, and what his chain of command thought of him. I knew if this was an isolated incident or one of many. I knew if he was invaluable to the team...or not. And I cared about him.

I was not only his judge but also his public defender.

Of course, there are bad apples on every tree. They come equally from every yard, some from the mean streets of deprived urban areas, some from pastoral small towns and farms, and an equal number from upscale homes. No one can predict a person's character based on where he came from; it is developed through his upbringing and sense of right and wrong. In fact, those from less privileged families often had a stronger desire to succeed and more to lose if they didn't make it in the Navy. They had already experienced, in blood and bruises, the tripwire between good and bad...and understood that doing the right thing sometimes had a cost. A few sailors had traits that were not compatible with the military; there was not much we could do for or with them. They were a quickly separated.

In the days of sail, the captain met with the crew under the mainmast on Sunday morning before divine services to put out the word, praise those who had done well, and punish those who had not. Consequently, this ceremony came to be known as "mast." I too held mast at the foot of *Vandy*'s mast, weather permitting. A couple of junior sailors would drag a heavy wooden podium up a few flights of steep ladders to be used as my judicial bench. The location and formal staging imparted a solemnity to the process, though it paled to earlier times when they hanged sailors from the mast after mast. It inhibited a convivial atmosphere, and was open and public.

Mast was the only evolution on the ship we all knew was going to be unpleasant, from start to finish and for some time after—not just for the sweating sailor, at attention in his dress uniform waiting to hear his fate, but also for the entire chain of command, including me. To get to this point, we had all failed in some way.

This was the one evolution on the ship that Jenna was not welcome to attend. There could be no smiles or petting here. Her piece would come later.

The sailors who stood at attention before me fidgeted, eyes downcast, sweating in their white uniforms and clenching their "Dixie cups"—the white hat made famous on the Cracker Jack box—until it crumpled. Most were good men who had made a mistake. I heard from everyone in their chain of command: the work center supervisor, the chief, the division officer, and the department head. They reported on their sailor's performance and explained why he was here. I knew this stuff already, but it was important for the sailor to hear what his chain of command thought about him. And also for that chain of leaders to think through what we might have done to prevent being here. Master Chief got his say, as did the XO. The sailor was allowed to have character witnesses or anyone else he wanted to speak on his behalf, but this was rare. His primary character witnesses were his chain of command lined up opposite him.

Then it was the sailor's turn to talk, to explain, to give his side of what happened. Rarely did anyone claim innocence; this was not a court where a lawyer weaved law statutes into a handsome verdict. We were driven by facts and common sense, and I believe I always knew the truth of what had happened. The sailor almost always expressed remorse at letting himself and his shipmates down, and often shed tears of shame. This on a ship of macho males, in a public forum.

It was uncomfortable for all of us.

But I did not move and kept my face a hard mask. The only other time I saw tears was when I had to inform someone, in the privacy of my cabin, of a death in their family. These strong emotions underscored each sailor's commitment to the team, and his understanding that he was facing stern consequences for letting the group down.

I came to mast with lots of facts and a sense of what "sentence" I would hand out, but was sometimes swayed by the chain of command or the sailor standing before me. I was stern, not loud but leaning in toward him, staring hard into his eyes, showing my anger and disappointment.

I passed judgment.

The Master at Arms ordered the sailor to cover (put his Dixie cup on) and salute.

I slowly returned his salute, holding his eyes until he was dismissed.

After mast there was none of the camaraderie that was normal when a group assembled, no socializing; all were dismissed. I always walked about the decks afterward, alone, unapproachable, emitting a prickly force field. I wanted everyone to understand that we didn't take this lightly, that we had all lost a little, that we had to lead sailors toward success rather than to mast. We posted mast results in the Plan of the Day for all to read, not to embarrass anyone but to show accountability and to head off rumors of inequitable justice.

I sought out sailors in their workplace a few weeks after they had been to mast. On one occasion, I visited a young sonar technician who had interrupted his promising career by going UA (unauthorized absence) for a few days. We headed down to find Petty Officer Caldwell[4] in the sonar equipment room. Yes, "we." I always took Jenna with me, an instantaneous furry stress reliever.

I carried Jenna down the ladders, this space being a couple levels below the main deck. She knew better than to squirm, but her body was rigid as we made our way deeper into the ship. There was nothing about being carried that she liked. We finally arrived at an equipment room dominated by floor-to-ceiling gray computer cabinets, fluorescent egg yolk-yellow overhead lights adding to the room's extreme blandness. Caldwell came around from behind a cabinet and stopped in his tracks to stand at rigid attention, clearly shocked to see us in this remote location. I put Jenna down onto the sea-green rubberized matting, a short "hrumpff" expressing her displeasure at the bumpy ride down. I told him to stand at ease, but he remained taut.

Jenna looked around at a room she had not been in before, then walked directly over to Caldwell, who knelt and proffered his hand. She sniffed and sat facing him, looking at him without expression. He glanced at me, unsure of what to do with this suddenly sociable dog. I nodded, and he petted her. Jenna did not react, but sitting still for that few minutes was her equivalent of arching her back in pleasure. She then stood and began her survey of the room, and Caldwell stood too. His eyes were crinkled, and a smile touched his lips despite standing in front of the Commanding Officer who had recently demoted him.

Jenna had put him at ease. The sailor who had stood ramrod straight before me was calmer and better able to talk. I told Caldwell that his mistake did not define him, here or in his future life. I believed in him, I trusted him, and we would help him to succeed. I then shared a failure of mine, a long menu to choose from. I went to mast on my first ship as an ensign for a prank gone bad, and I was fortunate to have had a captain who taught me a lesson without ruining my career before it had even started.

Petty Officer Caldwell admitted that he had gone UA on purpose, that family problems combined with a demanding work schedule made him "lose it." This admission was important to clear the air, enabling both of us to turn the page and focus on getting him back on track. No one claimed innocence at this point. Most who went to mast didn't look back, and many went on to successful careers—including Caldwell.

Some even made it to command!

Jenna was *all* about keeping cats in bags, or healing the scratches as soon as possible if the cat got out. She had made a difference for one sailor, as she had for so many others.

I was reminded that captains, too, are subject to judgment and penalty.

The phone rang; it was the outside line. Jenna looked up, eyes not making it past half-mast. I finished the sentence on an evaluation and picked up after four rings. It was my buddy Scott, friends since we commanded minesweepers together in South Texas. He now worked as an executive assistant for a high-ranking Admiral. As such, he knew everything the Admiral knew...which was a lot. He also knew that I didn't get much Pentagon insider gossip way out here in Japan.

"Hey, man, how's life in the Fuckin' Forward-Deployed Naval Forces?"

"Good, Scott, livin' the dream!"

Jenna's eyes closed and she laid her chin down. Obviously this was going to be one of those mundane human interactions that lacked interesting stuff like butt sniffing and snacks.

Boring.

"Do you know what you're doing next? You gotta get to DC, where the action is."

"Yeah, yeah. I hear you, Scott, but I am lovin' life here. Those minesweepers were great, but this is *so* much better. I can't believe they're paying me to do this...I would pay the Navy to be here!"

"OK, I get it. But it's gonna end at some point. And you have some ground to make up."

There was a short pause. "What do you mean...?"

"I heard that Slacker mentioned you the week after he got his fourth star. And not in a positive way."

Slacker.

My blood froze...or at least got cold enough that the tips of my fingers were suddenly numb.

"C'mon man, you're joking." I cleared my throat. "There's no way he even knows my name."

"Not what I heard. Apparently you, *and your little dog too*, made a lasting impression."

"That's bullshit! He seriously has nothing better to do than track some poor commander eight thousand miles away?"

"Dude, you better keep your head down and crawl on your belly to your next duty station. And get rid of that dog! Having her is extremely cool, but it ain't worth throwing away seventeen years of hard work."

"OK, OK...I hear you. But it's not that easy. She has become part of the crew."

"Whatever. Get a lizard like I had. You need to choose between that dog and your career. Gotta go. MyAdmiral is en route. See ya."

The phone clicked dead, and I slowly placed it in its cradle. As I released the phone, I realized that my palm had an indent. I stared straight ahead, eyes unfocused. My career had been going great. One of a handful promoted early to the rank of commander and in command ahead of my peers, I was on the fast track.

Could I throw all that away for a silly whim?

I looked over at Jenna, a red ball with snout tucked under her tail. Calm and detached, she worried only about what was happening today. No cares about tomorrow, she would deal with that as it came.

Hmpphh. Easy for her.

Maybe an alligator lizard would be a more suitable mascot, and we wouldn't have to worry about all the drama.

Or special preparations for gun shoots.

Or tracking down four-legged escapees.

"What's up?" Unusual cooperation to stay for a picture

Seaman Jenna, US Navy

Seaport

Jenna in Corpus Christi

Cruising (Corpus Christi)

In the captain's chair

Under the weather (and someone's blanket)

Jenna on the fantail

Kusumoto on bridge wing

Jenna at General Quarters with fire protection gear

Jenna in Captain's chair

Jenna in Captain's chair (when she was part of the crew)

Jenna visits Snips (engineers)

Wedding on the *Vandy*

At the beach (San Diego)

The crew reunites

Retirees visit *Vandegrift*

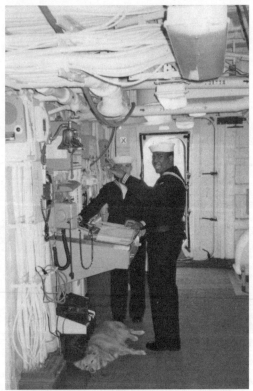

Jenna "standing guard" on the Quarterdeck

Jenna underway in retirement

Goodbye (final days)

17.

SHARKS AND SEALS

Sharks are like dogs.
They only bite when you touch their private parts.

— ROB SCHNEIDER in 50 First Dates

The ocean beckons to us, drawing populations close to coastlines and vacationers to beaches. There are few pleasures as calming as bobbing in a warm sea, salty water lightening the weight of worries as well as some earthly bulk. In the Navy we spend much of our lives on the sea, usually as passive observers transiting through its blue essence. We know there is a teaming world below us, but we only glimpse the few creatures that swim near the surface...mostly dolphins, whales, and flying fish. And sometimes sharks.

Sharks are abundant everywhere, the hunters and scavengers of the sea. We don't see them often, for unlike dolphins, they avoid getting close to large ships cutting through the water. But we know they are there, no matter where we sail. I have seen a giant whale shark swim past while at anchor off Oman, gentle but impressive. I saw huge sharks caught while moored in the port of Diego Garcia, and have seen pictures of Hector, the twenty-eight-foot hammerhead who ruled that harbor. There are great whites, the ever-present blues, tigers, hammerheads, and the one most feared by those at sea: the oceanic whitetip. Whitetips ravaged five hundred sailors after the USS *Indianapolis* was sunk during World War II, by far the largest shark attack on humans.

We might not have seen them, but sharks made their presence known. They sometimes attacked the sonar that we trailed behind the ship, slashing expensive modules. They follow ships to eat the biodegradable garbage thrown overboard. We all understood that, should we fall overboard, we would be just another bag of garbage to be consumed at the free Navy buffet. And not just us. We feared that Jenna would fall overboard, that despite her four-wheel drive, an unexpected wave combined with her leap-first personality would lead to disaster. Although her color was similar to that of the killer tomato, it would be nearly impossible to spot her small head among the waves in order to recover her. We couldn't bear to picture her becoming shark bait.

My mom must have also feared for Jenna, because a package arrived with a hot-pink canine life jacket. Jenna did not love it. More accurately, she despised it because it was too constricting and not her style. As usual, she prevailed and we eventually quit trying to force it on her. The life jacket got stowed in a locker, the equivalent of where you stashed that Christmas sweater from your dotty aunt. I didn't push for its continued use, as I feared it might trip her up at some critical juncture. I envisioned her falling over the side and bobbing in our wake, a drifting red-haired Nunn.

I have conducted search and rescues at night for sailors who fell overboard, who could tread water and yell to attract attention. We rarely found them despite many ships and aircraft searching for days.

If Jenna fell overboard at night, she would be gone for good.

I felt a trickle of fear every night when we were at sea. Just before taps I would search the ship for the little red head and take her up to my cabin, where she slept at night. Before she went to bed, I'd take her for a bathroom break. I would lug her up the ladder, then open the door to the exterior deck. It was usually pitch black. I'd put her down, and she would quickly ramble out of sight. This was the highest-level deck, running about two hundred feet from the bridge, past the gun, all the way to R2-D2. There were no lights, and no one was up there at this time of night. I alone had the dog watch. My tiny red-lensed flashlight illuminated a few feet ahead of me, barely piercing the pitch-black darkness. Red light did not ruin our ability to see at night... nor did it help much.

As the ship pitched and rolled as the minutes ticked by, I would start to fidget. There are lifelines surrounding the exterior decks of a ship, fencing made of wire and stanchions to prevent *people* from falling overboard. These two lines are placed at heights of two and four feet. This was convenient for Jenna, who would extend her head until her neck was pressed tight against the lower line. She could easily fall through those two-foot gaps, should a wave smack the ship at an inopportune time. Calling her, well, you know by now that she came when *she* was ready. One time, I walked around to find her and instead found the steel refueling rig with my head. Jenna finally trotted into my small red circle of light, no doubt wondering at the loud swear words.

Sailors do sometimes get to swim in the ocean, despite the risk from finned carnivores. Swim call was a favorite way to relieve the boredom of being at sea for a long time. The ship stops in the middle of the ocean and lets the crew go swimming. Sounds simple, but it is not. This is a rare and special evolution that few sailors get to experience. The Navy hierarchy frowns upon swim call because it is considered too risky for the morale payoff.

I agreed with the Navy brass. I felt the risk to my sailors, to my shipboard family, outweighed the reward. I based my decision, and defended it against requests for overturn, upon my own swim call experiences. As a young officer I was at sea for 122 straight days in the Indian Ocean. It was a hot, turbulent, boring four months. I blinked like a mole when I came up from the boiler room and realized I was looking at the sky for the first time in days. The captain held two swim calls during this time, and they did increase crew morale. After a few straight months of utter boredom, any change was welcome.

I had the bad luck to be the Officer of the Watch on the bridge for the first swim call. We conducted a safety brief and set the engineering plant so we wouldn't chop up anyone in the screws (propellers) or suck them into a sea chest (water intake). We informed all hands that we would sound one blast on the ship's whistle if we sighted a shark, and stationed sentries armed with rifles in a small boat and on the ship. This was before Shark Week and the fascination with these toothy predators, but the menacing soundtrack from *Jaws* was playing in our heads: *Duh Dunt...Duh Dunt...Duh Dunt...Duh Dunt.*

I stood on the bridge wing watching the crew leap off the side and swim around, enjoying a warm bath in the Indian Ocean, then climbing back aboard via the cargo netting draped over the side. After about twenty minutes we sighted sharks, and I blew the ship's whistle.

Imagine more than a hundred guys instantaneously transitioning from treading water to frenzied dash. It looked like the Olympics as each one tore through the water, frothing the water to a white foam. The image of terrible jaws just inches from their legs [DUH DUNT, DUH DUNT, DUH DUNT], the feeling that they were about to be pulled under by a giant man-eater, drove them into a mad rush. From my vantage I didn't see a shark approaching anyone; the thrashing cavalcade had frightened off the sharks. I was more concerned that one of our sentries would get an itchy finger and accidentally pick off one of the swimmers. We were on a bobbing ship, and no one got much range practice.

Everyone got aboard, hearts racing but sporting big smiles at having cheated death. The captain, his heart no doubt also beating fast, decided to move the ship away from those sharks.

A few hours and fifty miles later, we held a second swim call. Those who had been on watch during the previous swim got a chance to participate. The safety rail on the flight deck went down, nets went over, and we leaped in. I swam with my buddies away from the ship, perhaps one hundred yards.

It was amazing to tread water, nothing below for hundreds of fathoms, the water clear with a slight green hue, small particles sparkling below like suspended glitter. The ship looked so different from this perspective, large and loud, out of place. Treading water, I wondered what swam below me out of sight. The Indian Ocean teems with life. I have seen schools of dolphins that filled the entire horizon, many thousands strong. Sea snakes floated everywhere in this area of the world, yellow venomous ribbons sunning on top of the water.

Our time in the water was short-lived. A huge shark swam under the ship and then just beneath someone treading water.

Ship's whistle!

I swam faster than an Olympic medalist and scaled the rigging as if boarding a pirate ship with cutlass in mouth.

So I had conflicting emotions as I deliberated whether we should hold swim call on *Vandy*. I knew how cool swim call was, a life experience that few could add to their bucket, but in the end I was the frumpy parent whose answer was "no." Twenty years later I still second-guess myself, playing the futile game of "shoulda, woulda, coulda." There have been deaths during swim calls, but they are rarer than the chance to swim in the middle of the ocean. Sorry, boys!

Sharks are threatening for sure, but seals are more deadly. Navy SEALs, that is. We practiced a rare tactic during Foal Eagle, one that might have been required should the balloon have gone up; we embarked a SEAL platoon to insert into a simulated hot spot in Korea. This was long before the public became enamored of this elite group of naval warriors. The SEALs brought their small craft and lots of weapons, and the crew got a kick out of seeing their cutting-edge weaponry.

Late at night, cold seas churning, we approached the dark coast. I extinguished all lights, including our navigational beacons. We were completely dark. We had set EMCON (emissions controlled), so we used only our small commercial radar and no voice communications. This was dangerous, like driving a car down a dark road at night with no headlights. We were going to feel our way into the South Korean drop zone.

We communicated with the SEALs by blinking Morse code through an infrared light at the top of the mast. The standard operating procedure (SOP) was to approach to five miles from land and launch the SEALs' boats. But in the cold and choppy weather, each mile in their small rubber crafts added danger and time to their mission. I decided to lessen their risk by increasing our own and took the ship inside of three miles, chancing collisions with small craft we could not see and that could not see us.

Three miles sounds like a long distance, but to a large ship navigating an unfamiliar coast—at night—it was tight. I had navigated near to shore a lot while commanding a minesweeper in Europe and was more comfortable being close-in than most of my captain peers. Visibility was good, and there was little wind. The only sound on the bridge was the quartermaster ticking off our location and distance to our objective, all of us aware of the tangible threat from unknown shoals, unfamiliar currents, and unseen craft.

We launched the SEALs, and they whizzed off to their secret mission.

The next night we returned, darkened, creeping in close again, alert to threats real and simulated. We saw an answer to our infrared signal, and I turned the ship to face the open ocean for a quick getaway. We recovered the SEALs, then sprinted out of danger.

SEALs are the top Special Forces operators in the world, renowned for their courage and tenacity under fire. They have always been *that* good, but they are now the darlings of the press after their public successes. They got Bin Laden and everyone else they came up against, only failing once...against their most deadly predator, "ORCA." The On-demand Reactive Canine Attack.

SEALs conduct periodic exercises with Navy ships in port to test our ability to detect and deter a swimmer attack. These can be dangerous. A good friend was killed in an accident during one of these drills. The SEALs, I must admit, were always successful even though we knew they were coming. Swimming underwater, making no bubbles, in the dark or twilight, they could attach something to the hull or even find a place to get on board without a hint of their presence.

Vandy was "attacked" by a clandestine SEAL platoon one night in Yokosuka, Japan. They approached underwater and surfaced at *Vandy*'s stern. The team boarded silently, slowly raising themselves onto the dark flight deck. At least it was silent to human ears, but we had the ORCA system in standby mode—sleeping—on the quarterdeck forty feet away. Despite her less-than-prime readiness status, Jenna heard the first swimmer as he slithered over the rail.

Jenna jumped to her feet and ran toward the intruders, barking and snarling, taking away the key element of surprise and winning the day for the surface warriors. The SEAL team leader was grudging in his praise—they don't like to lose—admitting defeat but stating that we "cheated" by having a watchdog on board.

We only got boarded one other time.

The US Navy had been intercepting and boarding vessels to ensure compliance with UN sanctions since the invasion of Kuwait. I know because I wrote the guidance for our intercepts of Iraqi ships. Although interactions with merchants were not as fiercely contested, we still went armed and ready for whatever we might find. While working with the Japanese task group, Rear Admiral Sakaue decided he wanted his crews to take advantage of our expertise. *Vandy* acted as a merchant ship, the target of Japanese naval interceptors. We prepared a few surprises for them, maneuvering when they wanted *Vandy* to stay on course and practicing a bit of maritime civil disobedience. Just enough to make it challenging.

Japanese forces are always painstakingly prepared; everyone knows the plan and their exact part to play. Reference A was their refueling precision and teamwork during RIMPAC. They were well rehearsed for this new mission but perhaps not prepared for the unexpected. And a surprise is what they got. Their team chief led the way to the bridge. He was fully dressed out in a flak jacket, life jacket, helmet, boots, and drawn sidearm. His body weight was probably 140 pounds, but he was wearing an additional forty. They were dressed to portray strength to obtain instant cooperation from a civilian crew, and if that didn't work, they were ready for tactical action.

But they had not planned for ORCA as part of their intricate tactical takedown.

Jenna had the dog watch, which meant her eyes might have been closed, but she *was not sleeping* despite her rhythmic breathing. When the bridge door opened, her eyes popped open, and she reacted violently when bulky strangers entered the bridge. Barking aggressively, her hair stood on end all the way from her neck through the curve of her tail, which was pointed straight back rather than the normal curl. We were startled by her intensity, but the Japanese team was stunned. They backpedaled quickly, looking to us for help.

We grabbed Jenna, who struggled to get free as she continued to bark, ready to defend the bridge. We scooped her up and took her below so the drill could continue.

Our Warrior Princess.

18.

PERFECTING THE INU (DOG)

For much of my life, the Navy
was the only world I knew.
It is still the world I know best and love most.

— SENATOR JOHN McCAIN

We came to love Japan! Many of the *Vandy* crew, those same sailors who were dead set against the move to Japan, stayed for many years. Some are still there, having married Japanese women and remained for their entire careers. Sailors and their families appreciated the small-town attributes—honesty, attentive helpfulness, and a lack of crime—that persisted in even the most crowded parts of Japan. They could let their children roam without worrying about their safety, and a lost wallet would be returned intact. On the confusing subway you would be helped, without asking, if you appeared the least bit bewildered. If the first person who saw you did not speak English, she found someone who did. Getting sailors to move to Japan was a challenge, but getting them to leave was even harder.

We had a great relationship with the Japanese Navy, but our enthusiasm went far beyond that. Japan is a beautiful country, bathed in cherry blossoms or snow and presided over by Mount Fuji, a mystical and transcendent icon. Everything is in its place, on time, compact but functional, *perfected*. But the real treasure, the essence of this perfection, is the people. Complex beneath a quiet exterior, eager to please and unable to utter *iie* (no) to a request, introverts who go out of their way to help strangers, the people are the reason so many sailors decide to stay in Japan for the rest of their lives. We learned to be careful in conversation, as the slightest suggestion would be acted upon with speed and vigor, regardless of the cost. Casually admire a piece of fruit and you would receive some as a gift despite their exorbitant cost. And somehow the flavor was concentrated in a perfect compact replica.

Jenna was a prime example of Japanese skill, precision, and dedication. The Shiba Inu is one of the most ancient canine breeds. The Japanese worked for twenty-five centuries to assemble a big dog squeezed into a small package; for comparison, the USA is on its fourth century as a nation. They refined this breed to possess traits desirable in both humans and dogs. Shibas are independent and reserved toward strangers but loyal to those who earn their respect. They are a Spitz breed, a smaller version of the famous dog Hachikō, who waited for his master at the train station for years. The breed standard is a spirited boldness, a good nature, and an unaffected forthrightness, which together yield dignity and natural beauty. Jenna had loads of spirited boldness, but her cooperation and camaraderie genes were deficient.

Jenna was quiet, catlike, eschewing company and fastidiously self-grooming. She sought high places to sleep and had an overwhelming desire to go on liberty—alone—to sniff out life's adventures. She fit in perfectly with a crew bent on seeing the world. Jenna held few people dear; most she regarded as mere associates. I can picture her to this day, lying on her stomach, back legs splayed and front paws elegantly crossed, calmly studying her surroundings. Her Cheshire smirk suggested happiness, yet was the epitome of the inscrutable Oriental countenance that betrayed nothing to the outside world.

Japan and the Japanese are not perfect. But their sense of honor and propriety, their shrines and gardens, their friendship, cars, and *dogs* approach perfection. Of course, every city and province is different. We were fortunate to make port visits to Shimoda, Yokohama, Naha, and Kagoshima.

We hosted John Vandegrift,[5] General Vandegrift's nephew, for our visit to Kagoshima on the island of Kyushu in southern Japan. We passed Sakurajima volcano, which reminded me of Diamond Head crater in Hawaii, as we sailed toward the harbor. But this volcano was active, as there was white smoke rising from its crater. The harbor pilot was also awestruck and stated that this fume was a rare and auspicious occurrence.

John was standing on the bridge wing surveying the city as it unfolded in front of us. Jenna was sitting near him just beyond arm's length, her nose twitching as she scanned the water and surrounding banks. John was standing stiffly, hands on the rail, lost in his thoughts. His eyes remained fixed on the valley between the green mountains that led to the city. As I joined him at the handrail, he came out of his reverie and his eyes slowly focused on me as he returned to the present. He smiled wanly and shook his head.

"Not sure if I told you, but I've been here before," he said.

Rather amazed at this revelation, never mentioned during our many hours together, I turned toward him with a quizzical look.

"No, I don't think you did."

"Yep, more than fifty years ago. I led a bombing run into Kagoshima during the war." He was looking down at his shoes and slowly raised his eyes to meet mine. His lips were pressed together, and his knuckles were white as he gripped the rail. I saw a swirling mix of emotions on his face: pride...loss...regret.

That had been so many years ago, before I was born. When the world was different. When terrible things had to be done. His bombing of this city was a speck on the meter of loss when compared to the atomic bomb that leveled nearby Nagasaki . But still, for this man and for this city, a terrible day of killing and dying.

The fact that my family originated from this prefecture added yet another dimension.

"John..." I hesitated, wondering what the right words were. "Thank you for your service. I know this trip must bring back some grim memories."

As he turned to leave, I grabbed his hand and pulled him into a half-hug. He looked at me, then attempted a smile as his head drooped.

I let him go and said, "Let's keep your previous visit just between us for now...."

He nodded, then gingerly climbed down the ladder from the bridge.

There were many news crews on hand for our arrival, along with the perfunctory handful of protesters. Even Japanese protesters were precise and polite. I could set my watch by when they started and stopped protesting each day, self-policed to remain in a small set-aside area within sight of the ship. They chanted just loudly enough to be heard within a limited area.

As in many ports, there was press interest. Japanese reporters always asked me the same three questions: Do you speak Japanese? (my answer was *sukoshi*, which means "a little"); how many generations since your ancestors arrived in the US? (*sansei*, third); and have you climbed Mount Fuji? (*iie*, no, not yet). But today we had a more outspoken group of correspondents.

"Who is USS *Vandegrift* named after?" Rather than say the general was a hero for defeating the Japanese at Guadalcanal, I stated that he was the Commandant famous for saving the Marine Corps as a service. I scanned the room and was glad that John Vandegrift was not here. It could have been awkward that we had brought a guest who had once bombed their city. Then I got an antagonistic question, at least for this society, from a reporter exhibiting the *unaffected forthrightness* of a Shiba.

"Why did you have a missile exposed when you entered the harbor; don't you think that is threatening?" He was talking about the blue-colored missile shape on the launcher that we staged as a prop whenever we entered a port.

I looked the reporter in the eye and asked, "Do you feel threatened?"

He winced, and I assumed our Fleet Public Affairs Officer (PAO) at my side did as well.

I took my tone down a notch. "It is not a real missile, just a replica for show. Our missiles are weapons of self-protection, and we displayed one to show support for our close ally, Japan."

After the session I was astounded when the PAO congratulated me on how I handled the provocative inquiry. I was happy to return to running a ship rather than dabbling in international relations.

The next morning, I took Jenna out for our morning stroll and was surprised to see a perfect spiral of towns-people queued up for ship tours—hundreds of them, even though tours would not start for another five hours. There were no ropes or other means of coordinating the long line of people, as we were not prepared for their early arrival or considerable numbers. But there they were, arranged in a complex spiral that optimized the confined pier space. There were no complaints, no line-cutters, no loud radios. Each person stood quietly and dispassionately, Shiba Inus in human clothing.

I fetched Jenna's leash and led her onto the pier. After she whizzed on some weeds near the brow, we approached the human helix. I could not understand what was being said, but I could see they were amazed to see a Japanese dog coming from an American ship. They pointed and the girls laughed behind their hands, and some of the children came up to pet her. Did she have a better rapport with these humans, a blood bond formed over twenty-five centuries?

Nope.

She kept her head raised high, pointed away from her suitors, and stood rigidly while they petted her.

We made some quick adjustments to begin tours early for our eager visitors. This same self-policed queue occurred every day, easing the burden of hosting more than a thousand enthusiastic visitors.

Our next port visit in Japan was to the Black Ship Festival in Shimoda, some 530 miles northeast.

Kagoshima is a southern city in the farm belt, while Shimoda is a smaller town near Tokyo that was settled in prehistoric times. The Black Ship Festival is an annual celebration of Japan opening to the West. Commodore Matthew C. Perry led a squadron of US Navy ships that paid calls in 1853 and 1854, resulting in a treaty with Japan that initiated trade. Commodore Perry's visits were true gunboat diplomacy, a show of superior force and technology to force Japan to open her doors after two hundred years of isolation. The Japanese labeled these foreign ships "black" because of their tar-covered sides and the dark smoke they expelled.

The Navy still sends ships to Shimoda, but now it is to support a magnificent festival. Every ship vies to be a participant in this lavish three-day party held just a short sail from our home port. There are golf tournaments, sports competitions, fishing excursions, and sumptuous dinners. It is a superlative opportunity to celebrate our close relationship and to honor our cultural differences. And to raise a sake box[6] in a toast.

Skip Triplett, Tony Fortson, and I played in the Black Ship golf tournament. Land in Japan is precious, especially near the sea, so the golf course was cut into the mountains. Instead of marching down typical long horizontal fairways, we found ourselves clambering up and down severe slopes. We had caddies, delicate ladies dressed in heavy clothing and large floppy hats. It was impossible to determine if they were in their thirties or sixties. Our golf bags were put into individual carts that rode upon a track that followed each hole, an ingenious system I had not seen then or since. One of the ladies pushed a button, and the cart proceeded to the next stop.

After watching us play a few holes, these ladies had an accurate analysis of our golf games. Too bad they didn't speak English; they could have provided valuable tips even though they had probably never played a round due to golf's prohibitive cost in Japan. I asked for a 6-iron on the third hole but was handed a 5-iron. I smiled kindly at her imperfect English and handed the club back to her, repeating, *"Roku, kudasai"* ("Six, please"). She shook her head. OK, she thought I was under-clubbing for this shot. I took her advice, and she was correct.

We assembled in the clubhouse after the round to be served *biru* (beer) and curry. Japanese curry is somewhere between traditional curry and English stew, a light brown non-spicy gravy with carrots and potatoes served over short-grain rice. We bonded within the universal brotherhood of golf, the never-ending quest for momentary excellence in an intractable game. As we ate, I perused the wall of prizes. In the US, the top few golfers win trophies and golf gear. But here there were prizes of every sort piled five feet high. It was a mini-Mount Fuji of golf clubs, hefty golf bags, foodstuffs, clothing, and lots more.

They started handing out prizes. Although I didn't have a great day, I did have the best score in our group and *was* the captain of the ship. Surely rank had its privileges. Those expensive drivers sure looked good. I was called up, there was applause, and I was handed a box of laundry detergent. Big winner! Lots of us got detergent; no one went home without a prize.

Skip, who had a rough day, was awarded an expensive putter. Whaaaat?!?

Oh well, we had a great time commiserating in broken English with our new friends over the tribulations of our shared golf insanity. The more biru we toasted each other with, the better we communicated. When it was time to depart, our new friends embraced us as if we were longtime neighbors. This was not an anomaly; we found the Japanese people to be overwhelmingly *good-natured*.

It's a trait that they bred into the Shiba Inu. At least most of them. Jenna tended toward the introverted side, with little need to please others.

The formal Black Ship reception the next night was something to behold. As always, our Japanese hosts had gone above and beyond. There were stations of food set up in an extraordinary garden overlooking the sea, the *Vandy* visible at anchor a few miles offshore. *Many* stations, so many that they were never crowded despite hundreds of guests in formal attire. We mingled among ambassadors, politicians, senior officials, Admirals and generals, and local VIPs.

My favorite was the tempura booth, where they deep-fried prawns and vegetables. Describing tempura as "deep-fried" does not do it justice. In Japan, tempura is an art that delivers crisp and light food without a hint of oiliness. *Oishi* (delicious). There were curry stations, soba and udon noodles, and a huge selection of sushi. Of course there was tea, warm or chilled sake, and lots of ice-cold biru. Everywhere I looked there was something beautifully crafted and gracefully served.

In the middle of this overwhelming food festival was a massive ice sculpture, a leaping dolphin with waves of ice bearing hundreds of huge pink prawns, oysters on the half shell, clams, and many kinds of fish. I took a prawn, and a replacement was inserted into the ice before I could even take a bite.

Oops! I was surprised the shrimp was much softer than expected.

It was raw.

I got it down but was careful to select the cooked ones during future grazing. I have a theory that there is one bad piece of seafood at every function, and I didn't want to be the unlucky soul who got sick.

At sunset we heard "Colors" from our ship in the harbor below. We came to attention, facing our ship, proud and slightly buzzed as the Stars and Stripes was lowered. The ship's exterior lights blinked on, the up-and-over string of lights running from stem to stern illuminating the ship. A light breeze ruffled the ocean, inserting small white commas onto the darkening surface, the distant ship miniature against the purple shades of dusk. Evening twilight is that extraordinary time when darkness overcomes light, fiery orange giving way to deepening purple hues and then fading to black. That time when the day is done, and we look back on what we've accomplished and ahead to another day with renewed hope.

I looked often to find the ship during the night, her presence a beacon of freedom and international commitment. It was a perfect evening, presented with dignity in a setting of natural beauty, indulged by the world's most magnificent hosts. We were proud to be there, honored to continue supporting a country we opened to the West and rebuilt after World War II.

We rode water taxis back to the ship after we finished consuming as much food and drink as we could hold. It was a short ride, close to shore and shielded from winds and seas. Of course, after a night of raw seafood and strong drinks, the ride proved more upsetting than usual. One officer was quieter than his liberty mates, the glow from four-star food and drink fading fast. Once on the ship, he hurried to his rack, hoping to sleep off the growing unease in his stomach.

Sweat broke out on his brow, followed by a sour tang in his cheeks.

He jumped up, but realizing that he would never make it to the head, he heaved the contents of his stomach into the tiny sink in his stateroom. He tried to wash it down, but his sink backed up. He couldn't leave it like that, the stench would make him hurl again and his roommate would return soon. Just looking at the chunky brown soup curdling in his sink made him retch. He had to take care of it now. He stumbled out of his room, found a plunger, and wobbled back.

Fighting nausea, holding his breath and turning his head, he viciously plunged the sink. A satisfying *pop*, and the sink cleared.

Simultaneously he heard a bellow from the adjacent stateroom. Peering into the passageway, he saw his neighbor, dripping a pungent salad of seafood and gastric juices, dashing to the head to wash off the unexpected discharge.

Unbeknownst to him, the drainpipes from the two staterooms merged into a common drain. As the other officer brushed his teeth, his sink erupted with a stinking volcanic plume of half-digested oysters and beer, drenching him from head to belt. He never found out how this catastrophe happened.

Until now.

19.

NAVY'S CHIEF GETS A FURRY SURPRISE

Any commander who fails to exceed his authority
is not of much use to his subordinates.

— ADMIRAL ARLEIGH BURKE

The ship cut a straight line through the indigo sea, our white wake the only blemish on its smooth surface. The southern sun reflected off the water, creating countless sparkles across the blue expanse. Beneath this reflective icing the water was crystal clear near the surface, gradually turning a dark blue as it reached the deepest depths of our planet. It was the polar opposite of the bitter conditions we had recently endured in Korea, where early spring had felt like deep winter—at least in this Hawaii boy's opinion. As I sat on the bridge wing soaking up the warmth of these tropical seas, the soju-reboot of a frozen boat crew seemed a world away.

Vandy had sailed south to join the rest of the *Kitty Hawk* strike group for exercise Tandem Thrust, a large-scale US and Australian exercise performed in the waters around Guam. Those waters run deep. Real deep. The Marianas Trench is the deepest part of any ocean, reaching a depth of almost seven miles. For comparison, Mount Everest, Earth's highest peak, climbs 5.5 miles above the ocean.

In the midst of this exercise the Navy ordered our strike group to deploy immediately to the Arabian Gulf. Iraqi MiG-25 jets had crossed into the no-fly zone to exchange missiles with US F-14 fighters. The President wanted more firepower to enforce the Operation Southern Watch no-fly zone over Iraq. *Vandy*'s participation in the deployment was in limbo because we had already been away from home port for more than a month, and ships' deployments were limited to six months, which meant that we could not stay in the Gulf as long as the rest of our strike group.

We were going, we were not going, going, not going...

Commodore Ferguson sent a message to Admiral Keating, our Strike Group Commander, reporting that I was eager for *Vandy* to accompany the strike group to the Middle East. Hmmmm, I didn't remember saying that but understood the commodore was attempting to make me look good to the boss. Looking good to an Admiral could not hurt, especially with Admiral Blacker hanging out in the dark alleys of my mind. After a few days of deliberation, as the crew swung on the hook as to whether we would make an unexpected (unwelcome) deployment to the Gulf, the Admiral decided we didn't have enough time left on our deployment meter.

Too bad, so sad. Cheers erupted!

We would still be away from home for six months, but at least we wouldn't be cutting holes in the Arabian Gulf and fighting sandstorms.

Amid this uncertainty, the Chief of Naval Operations—the Navy's *Top Dog*—visited the strike group. Being on a smaller ship, this normally would not have impacted us. But once again, Commodore Ferguson was looking to shine a spotlight on us. Kind of surprising after he and the Admiral had observed my pirate crew, and Jenna, while we refueled from the aircraft carrier. At his suggestion, the CNO decided to visit a frigate rather than stay on the aircraft carrier or visit a larger cruiser.

A frigate...that was us.

CNO and his wife would come over for a quick visit. Nothing against senior officers, but hosting them always added extra work. And risk. I wondered if this would be a four-star replay of Admiral Blacker's unpleasant visit and grimaced as a metallic bile suddenly assaulted my mouth.

My rule was that the ship be always maintained in good stead and that we should not expend extra effort preparing for VIPs. But this was not just any VIP, this was THE CNO. We took time during the ongoing exercise to ensure the ship was gleaming. Another standing rule was that Jenna spend time in solitary confinement, i.e., napping in a stateroom, whenever we had senior leaders onboard. There was no reason to instigate undue questions or concerns. We weren't really hiding her... OK, maybe we were.

Visit day arrived. The sun was out, but the wind whipped whitecaps across this eastern edge of the Philippine Sea. We turned to put the wind off the bow to help the helicopter hover and land. Admiral Jay Johnson and his wife, Garland, debarked wearing inflatable life vests and cranial helmets, ducking to avoid the blades as they walked to the hanger. The CNO was tall and slim, and a ready smile had permanently creased his cheeks. Garland was clearly more than a placeholder. Blond and pretty, she projected an alpha wave of her own. We did the perfunctory greeting in the helo hanger, got their flight gear off, and I led them to the wardroom. En route the CNO was gracious and interested, shaking hands with all the sailors standing at rigid attention as we passed.

I always requested that visiting Admirals approve a few medals. Well, not always; I didn't ask Admiral Blacker. Those Flag medals wouldn't count against my quota, and receiving a medal from the CNO would be a special honor for my best performers. We were also getting him to re-enlist sailors, another rarity. *Vandy* was taking full advantage of CNO's visit.

The ship's leaders were stuffed into the wardroom, standing at attention in preparation for the CNO's arrival. When we entered the small wardroom, I escorted Garland to my chair at the head of the table, and she had a cup of coffee while her husband signed paperwork. Of course, the CNO does not travel without an entourage. He was accompanied by his Executive Assistant (EA), a senior captain who was on track to become an Admiral himself, as well as a lieutenant aide-de-camp—all of them wearing the gold braiding that signals military royalty. As I watched CNO good-naturedly sign papers, our well-laid plan unraveled.

The most critical moment of Jenna's time on board happened without fanfare or premonition. In my mind it always plays out in slow motion, every detail etched into my brain. The door that led to the officers' staterooms opened, and everyone turned to see who was arriving late. CNO's EA and my Navigator Dave Richardson, standing beside the door, looked down and did double takes. The EA whipped his head around and hissed to Dave, "You have a fuckin' dog aboard?!?!"

In trotted Jenna, somehow free of her restriction, ready for a nap in *her* wardroom. She walked right past the CNO, who flinched and smudged his signature, not expecting anything on four legs and perhaps thinking a bold rat had sauntered in. Jenna confidently walked the length of the table, tail curved into a C onto her back, directly to Garland. She commenced her Zen routine, a formal method of begging that looked like a ritualistic offering to the Sun. Jenna rose on her hind legs, put her front paws together and pumped them as if in a gallop while making a wavering howl. This is called the "Shiba scream." Even more astonishing for this independent soul, she then placed both paws onto Garland's lap.

The room was frozen, both crew and visitors aware that some precarious boundary had been crossed, that we were in the realm of never-been-seen-before.

Never.

Ever.

Garland bent down and petted Jenna, then looked up with a huge grin.

"Jay, they have a dog!"

Jay—I mean the CNO—had already figured that out.

I have always wondered what Admiral Johnson, the leader of the Navy whose every action conveyed significance and consequences, thought at that moment. What implications he weighed, what courses of actions he considered right then and after he returned to the *Kitty Hawk*. But he was a cool fighter pilot, continuing as if nothing had happened.

Garland stroked Jenna for a few minutes, and incredibly Jenna let her.

Had Jenna smoked out the true power and latched onto the Johnson household Alfa Leader?

The rest of the visit went well, a blur of awarding medals, re-enlisting sailors, and the CNO speaking to the crew. I showed him the best ship in the Navy, and he shook hands with many sailors...all proudly wearing red ball caps. The two hours he spent on board went quickly, and before long I was waving goodbye as their helo took off.

I didn't know what the CNO was considering, but two outcomes from his visit seemed likely. Outcome #1 was that he would get back to the aircraft carrier and give Admiral Keating a ration of shit: *Do you know about this dog? What kind of strike group are you running? Get rid of her ASAP!* The fallout would be that we would lose Jenna, *Vandy*'s reputation would take a dive, and my career would dead-end. Something that Admiral Blacker was already working on. The alternative was that the CNO would do nothing, that he—or his wife—would decide that a dog couldn't hurt. That he would not mess with a ship operating at a high level with extraordinary morale.

While we hoped for outcome #2, it seemed unlikely that the CNO would open the door for Navy ships to enlist dogs.

We waited for the NAVADMIN, the message the CNO sends to the entire Navy setting policy and guidelines. Surely, he would shore up this gap in Navy regulations that allowed mascots.

But he never did. We never got any feedback at all.

I considered this as the Chief of the Navy's blessing to keep Jenna on board.

Jenna stayed. We also kept our red ball caps.

Even today, decades later, I can see Jenna in high definition, trotting into the wardroom and upstaging the Chief of Naval Operations.

20.

IF THE NAVY WANTED YOU TO HAVE A SPOUSE... IT WOULD HAVE ISSUED YOU ONE

Dear Lord, give me greatness of heart to see,
The difference between duty and his love for me.
Give me the understanding, so that I may know,
That when duty calls he must go;
And, Dear Lord, when he goes out to sea,
please bring him home safely to me.

— Navy Wife's Prayer

Navy life is tough on relationships. Think of the person you love the most and are closest to, with whom you share a special bond—your spouse, or child, or parent, or best friend. The person you can't live without, who brings joy and happiness to your life, who brings an instant smile to your face when you see them. Your other half. Imagine you must leave that person for a week or a month. Is it hard to imagine going an entire month without seeing one another? What if you were cut off and could only hear that person's voice once or twice during that entire time? Now imagine you must deploy and leave them for six, or even nine, months. Being separated for more than half a year is hard to imagine, but that is what sailors and their significant others face. It is impossible to make your mind enter that realm, even when you are in the Navy.

The months before deployment felt like a looming prison sentence. Sailors and their families had to construct a brain cyber-wall to block out the upcoming separation. Pressure built day by day, internal barometers forecasting an oncoming front that would bring a leaden atmosphere with widespread tears. Even the family dog picked up the vibe and walked about with lowered ears, tail wagging at half-mast. We avoided talking about the deployment at home. We tried to ignore the impending separation, but it cast a growing shadow on our lives. Even joyful times were tinged with sadness, knowing that our time at home was dwindling, and the sweet times were ending. Each family strained to enjoy the autumnal blaze of their time together, each moment more precious as the deployment frost expanded, emotions sharpened to enjoy the waning warmth before the familial hearth grows cold.

To add to the stress, work on *Vandy* was getting more hectic as we wrapped up training, certifications, logistics, planning, and countless details required for our Odyssean-like journey. As that fateful day when the ship would pull away from the pier neared, clouds turned into storms bringing tearful downpours and thunderous arguments. A cold front moved in, each party angry, scared, and hardening their heart for the impending separation. Petty things normally ignored were instead magnified by the prism of future loneliness, by fears of having to deal with unknown issues without a partner, by the uncertainty of where the sailor would be going and what he would be doing.

Half of all Navy couples during this period eventually divorced. When a ship deploys, the overpowering thundercloud of stress and unhappiness is too much for many. Four percent of Navy marriages ended annually in 1999, which was higher than the civilian rate. Researchers[7] found that long Navy deployments increased the risk of divorce. Duh! Ninety-seven percent of divorces occurred after a return from deployment. There are so many bumps in the road of every marriage, so many unknowns when squeezing two people into one life, then add kids and bills, and subtract carefree weekends. Now stir in long Navy separations during which both sides harbor old grudges and form new ones, unable to work them out face-to-face, each overburdened and misunderstood, unable to hug and make things better. How does any relationship sail through these treacherous reefs?

Both the sailor and his spouse faced herculean tasks. The sailor would work day and night for six to nine months, seven days a week while at sea, often at tasks that didn't fit into the "fulfilling" category. The spouse was often the stronger partner in a Navy marriage, for she shouldered her family's burdens without the support of a crew around her. In 1999 she was not much better off than the lassies of old who watched from their widow's walk for a sign of sail on the horizon. No email and only a handful of phone calls—often in the middle of the night from ten time zones away—she was a "widow" running the family by herself. To be a good "Navy wife," she had to be as independent as a Shiba Inu, as fearless as a tiger shark, as flexible and multitasking as an octopus, and as strong as Rosie the Riveter. She had to be loving, sexy, and able to deal with plumbing issues. She dealt with teachers, neighbors, appliance repairmen, landlords...with shovels, garbage cans, cars and trucks, laundry, vacuum, car chamois...with swim meets, grocery shopping, veterinarians...with bills, taxes, car registration, and budgets. Today it is even more difficult, as women also deploy away from their families.

Families visited the ship every night in the weeks leading up to deployment to see their loved one while he was on duty—and *their* dog, Jenna. Most families in Japan could not have pets; they had to leave their pets behind in San Diego. Jenna was kept on the quarterdeck during the early evening to be available to children who came to see their fathers during dinner. She was on a long lead that allowed her to roam the fantail but precluded her from leaving the ship. She'd let out low grunt-gasps as she pulled to escape from this unwelcome restriction but would quickly determine that her efforts were in vain and sit glaring at the nearest sailor. After a few minutes, she would abandon her attempt to explore the base and trudge to her normal station, which was under the small desktop welded to the bulkhead. Sprawled out on her side, only her twitching ears revealed that she heard kids approaching. The watch stander warned families to be slow and careful with her to mitigate the persistent attention. When the first small hand gently petted her, she would slowly open her eyes and raise herself to half-mast, with front legs straight out but back legs still lying horizontal to the deck. Her face would betray nothing as she absorbed each child's devotion. The kids were anything but quiet as they took turns petting Jenna and whispering in her ear. Mothers watched, eyes glistening as their children reveled in that magical bond that humans and dogs have developed over millennia.

When the ship sailed, families lost their spouse, father, *and* their dog.

Holidays were the time when we missed family the most. Each Christmas tune brought a confusing mix of hope and despondency. The ship was not very festive; there was far more gray and black than green and red. With an all-male crew, no one felt the need for bows and candles, no potpourri, no eggnog, no gift exchange. Small plastic trees adorned the wardroom, chief's mess, and mess decks...plastic homages to Charlie Brown's pitiful tree. We only strung colored lights "up and over" the mast when we were in home port. That was the extent of our decorating, what some might graciously call minimalist.

This is not to say that we didn't have some special memories of our own over the holidays, and of course Jenna led the way. She was given a large bag of pig ears for her first Christmas on board, her version of a big box of maple candy. Jenna spent much of her time in the wardroom, as it was centrally located and people transited through at every hour of the day. But we had a process problem, the bag-o-ears was kept in the wardroom, but there was no procedure to control how many pig ears Jenna wolfed down.

We paid for this oversight.

Everyone wanted to make Jenna's tail wag, so there was a continuous parade of sailors who stopped by to give her a treat. Jenna could not turn down a tasty dried pig ear, no matter how many she was offered each hour. She gorged herself. Although no one witnessed the final act, it must have been like the projectile vomiting scene in *The Exorcist*. The wardroom, where the officers ate and relaxed, smelled like the sewage system had drained into it. We shampooed the carpets multiple times, but the sickly sweet smell was more enduring than a skunk's spray.

New carpet was Jenna's holiday gift to the wardroom.

Vandy was a ship full of men that smacked of testosterone and sweat, boasts and challenges, pride and competition. Not a place where weakness or failure was accepted or depression recognized. Every sailor was a warrior compelled to be tough and resilient in order to withstand the storms of life without breaking. Unless there was a death in the family or something of that magnitude, there was no outreach to "hold someone's hand." Of course, we all have times when the world is spinning at a different RPM than we are. Any sailor was free to talk to his chain of command, but that was rare in this macho environment. Senior leaders watched for telltale signs of extreme stress or depression, but often the inner workings were invisible to us.

The *Vandy* seemed small when at sea for months, confined by a vast moat, every hour planned and ordered. There was no place to escape the crowd. But there was one counselor on board who could be counted on to listen and keep a secret, whose loose lips sank no shipmates.

Dr. Jenna.

That's right. Aloof, anti-huggy Jenna provided a temporary wailing wall for the crew.

She did not have office hours, or even an office, but provided a walk-in trot-out service for her shipmates. Her sessions were not long; she didn't have *that* much patience. But she would lie down, ears erect, hearing if not understanding, letting a sailor unload his woes, complaints, anger, and sorrow without interruption or argument, letting him vent steam to ease the pressure. In Jenna's eyes we were all the same, our insignia was meaningless to her, and each of us was just another member of her pack.

We did *issue* a wife to one young sailor.

Sort of.

We hosted his wedding ceremony and a small reception on the fo'c'sle (the deck at the front of the ship) during our port visit in Hawaii. Captains on cruise ships marry people, but that doesn't happen in the Navy. At least during my twenty-five-year career, I only saw it once and never heard of another occasion. Of course, that *one time* happened to be on the *Vandy*. An eighteen-year-old, shiny new seaman apprentice named Ferland Antwine requested permission to get married. This was not an abnormal request; I got a number of these from junior sailors. I viewed marriages at such a young age with skepticism, having observed a high failure rate over the years. I sat each young man down and talked to him to ascertain if he was doing this in a rush and if he understood the long-term implications. Although I never disapproved a request, I did my best to dissuade hasty marriages.

Seaman Antwine was no different, but like most, he was wedded to his plan. And his fiancée had already flown from Houston to Hawaii, so there was little hope of a strategic pause to ensure they had thought it through. So all I could do was give him some advice and wish him well. At least I thought that was all I could do.

Matt LaPointe approached me with a "good idea." How about if we held a ceremony and small reception on the ship so there was a respectable audience? This would also save the young couple precious money. Matt was instrumental in the dog-mascot proposal...I was starting to see a trend in generating irregular ideas.

My answer was short and swift, and backed by the XO: No!

I didn't want to become a Vegas wedding chapel, making it easier for young sailors to get a quick and cheap wedding. But after a day of mulling it over, and with Matt's assertion that he would do all the work to make it happen, I relented. I was swayed by Matt's conviction and convinced by the love I saw in young Ferland's eyes.

Wedding day arrived, and the weather was sunny with a chance of brief showers—a standard Hawaiian day. Matt and the deck division had decorated the fo'c'sle, making an area dominated by the missile launcher, anchor windlass, and huge mooring lines as festive as possible. Not too many professional wedding planners have to deal with missiles, non-skid, and an utterly gray canvas. He draped a white curtain over my podium— the same one I used for captain's mast—from which to conduct the ceremony. The huge rubber mat from the quarterdeck was placed on the non-skid deck in front of the podium. A table, also draped in white, displayed a layer cake our cooks had baked and decorated.

This might not have sufficed for a Kennedy wedding, but it was nice for a warship. I'd never heard of a marriage on a Navy ship, much less seen one. It was the Fourth of July, and we were dressed in full white uniforms for this auspicious occasion. That meant we were in long pants and sleeves, and I was wearing my sword. We fanned ourselves to mitigate the voracious Hawaiian sun that beat down on us and the steaming metal deck that fried us from below as we waited for the prospective bride and groom. When the couple did not show up at the appointed time, we sought shade to avoid melting. There was joking that we would use the podium one way or another. Either I would preside over a wedding or hold mast for an absent seaman apprentice. I found out many years later that Ferland and Nikki had gotten cold feet and were thinking that marriage might not be wise. They hadn't seen each other in months and during that time had only talked once or twice while feeding quarters into a pay phone.

The couple finally arrived, and we took our places. Matt started wedding music on his boom box, and the couple walked past the missile launcher to the podium. The assembled crew stood in ranks, with many others watching from the bridge above. Jenna sat in the shade near the cake, tongue hanging out, no doubt wondering about this peculiar evolution. And if she would get any cake. There had been talk of Jenna being the ring bearer, but too many possible disasters had bounced around in my head. She might get the ring off and lose it—or charge off the ship to tour Hawaii.

I took the Antwines through the vows, and they agreed to all the right things. In just a few minutes they were married...sort of. This was a ceremony for their memories; I was not certified to marry anyone. Their marriage became official later that day when they found a church in Waikiki with a wedding in progress and persuaded the pastor to sign their marriage certificate. A year later they had an intimate ceremony at home for their families.

The Antwines, still married, joke that they got married three times and commemorate their life together with a three-day family celebration each year.

21.

THREE SHEETS
TO THE WIND

What shall we do with a drunken sailor,
Early in the morning?
Shave his chin with a rusty razor,
*Give 'im a hair of the **dog** that bit him,*
Put him in the bilge and make him drink it,
Put him in bed with the Captain's daughter.

— Traditional sea shanty

The full promise of the day was dead ahead. Morning arrived fresh and cool, the sea unruffled by even the slightest breeze. Mariners call it "shaded morning civil twilight," that dreamlike period between darkness and sunrise when everything is shaded in cool purple hues. Standing on the bridge we watched in wonder as the earth was reborn, as black night released its grip to set the stage for the sun's entrance. Stars hovered above the horizon, losing brilliance as the sky lightened. Watch standers welcomed a fresh new day, watching flying fish skim across the ocean to escape the menace of our white bow wave, flashes of gray-blue against the dark sea. The crew talked in low tones as the sun edged above the horizon.

Watch standers not only felt buoyant, they also began to feel hungry. The aroma of eggs, sausage, and potent coffee wafted up from the mess decks, rousing empty stomachs and signaling the end of their watch. Jenna was up and about, brought to life by breakfast bouquets drifting up from the galley. She stood at the cabin door, which was canine semaphore for me to let her out. She climbed the ladder up to the bridge and was greeted by the boatswain's mate, who set his coffee cup in a holder and bent to stroke her back. Jenna strolled out to the bridge wing, nose high and enjoying the fresh ocean breeze. She stuck her head between the lifelines to scan the horizon, watching the flying fish cruise across the wavetops. Her human shipmates couldn't see land yet, but she could already smell urban scents wafting past.

A palpable excitement gripped the ship as we prepared to "See the World," as promised in that famous Navy advertisement. We were primed to enter port, so the mood was like a Friday afternoon before a long weekend in Vegas. Hawaii had been a great port visit, but that had been months ago. As always, the crew had high hopes. Hope was not an esoteric inner warmth for us but a tangible collective mood as we looked forward to going ashore. As the ship glided toward land, the horizon was outlined by a faint glow, only a few lights from the tallest structures visible. Diffuse urban light gradually came into focus as we drew nearer, distinct lights sketching the city's form. Harbor lights blinked, beckoning us forward.

Red- and green-lighted buoys, flashing maritime street signs, marked a two-lane thoroughfare into the harbor. There were few headlights on the roads; it was too early for anyone except fishermen, bakers, and baristas. Mountains blocked the sun for a few minutes more, backlit cutouts as the sky lightened. We turned and cruised parallel to the shoreline, six miles offshore, waiting to rendezvous with the harbor pilot. Much of the crew was outside, leaning on the lifelines, smoking and joking, enjoying the cool air, their voices low but eager.

The Navy is the face of the US in the Western Pacific. With forces based in Japan, Guam, Singapore, and Australia, the Navy is always present. The United States remains in the public eye by sending ships to exercise with other nations and to conduct port calls throughout the area. By showing the American flag, we signaled our friendly support and won friends by doing public good deeds and injecting lots of cash into local economies. This was a good deal for everyone—sailors, locals, and the US.

I knew from my coffee sessions with hundreds of sailors that they joined the Navy to get away from a bad situation, to get an education, to serve their country, or to see the world. Seeing the world was payment for all the long hours, the low pay, and the family separation. It also educated us, broadening our minds and shaping our views to be based on a more global perspective. It opened our eyes to how the rest of the world lived and how good we had it. We saw that many fellow humans— including children—did not have the necessities of life. In our world of supermarkets crammed with every variety of food, restaurants and coffee shops on every corner, two-car garages, bottled water, free Wi-Fi, and frequent flyer miles, we cannot imagine how the rest of the world lives. Even water, that most basic necessity, is often in short supply.

There was a cadre of sailors who performed good deeds in every port. They were a diverse group of every race, creed, religion, and background. Each had a reason why they spent their treasured liberty time repairing orphanages, painting schools, or tutoring kids. The work was hands-on labor as the language gap prevented tutoring. They gave their time, energy, and sweat to help the poor in a foreign country that they would never visit again, doing work for people they would never meet. Each got to see a real part of another country or culture, and made life better for people in need. These humanitarian efforts built grassroots goodwill and support for the USA. Each of these sailors was not content just to *see* the world but took hands-on action to improve it.

Our visits to third-world countries made us appreciate our privileged way of life, our freedoms, our rights,
our security, and the everyday abundance that made our
lives easy in comparison to most. We came away with an
appreciation of what we had and were less apt to com-
plain about lukewarm food, a remote parking space, or
a middle seat on the plane.

But mostly, port visits were about fun.

"Join the Navy, See the World" was the Navy's most
successful slogan. The Navy conducts port visits around
the world, and those visits are one of its biggest draws.
Port calls are like Christmas to sailors. We worked
hard to visit the primo ports, looked forward to them
for months, kept them in our dreams, and then talked
about them for the rest of our lives. And with each year
those sea stories got bigger and better.

Back when we relied on wind to power our ships,
three "sheets" (lines) held the sail. If all three were loose
and flapping "into the wind" the ship was out of control,
staggering under the influence of waves and currents.
These days, someone staggering under the influence
of alcohol is, "three sheets to the wind." What did we
do with a drunken sailor? In 1999, his buddies bought
him another drink, clapped him on the back, and kept
going. That sounds appalling while sitting at home in a
sterile environment, sober and sane. But those were different times in faraway lands, long before temperance
was accepted in the fleet. When hundreds of sailors and
Marines went on liberty, there was bound to be a prob-

lem or three. Sailors committed far fewer crimes than civilians, but it only took one serious crime to erase the goodwill generated by a port visit. Most of these incidents happened late at night and involved the youngest sailors.

We set up tours in every port and paid half of the cost to encourage the crew to get out and see that part of the world. But many liberty hounds didn't make it past the harbor bars. They traveled around the world to...get drunk, often on overpriced, bland American beer. It was fun and bonding, and we usually didn't have to walk far to get back to the ship. A driving factor for the young guys was the eternal testosterone-driven quest to track down a local lady, despite odds that weren't any better than winning a scratch-off lotto.

What did the f-legged liberty hound do when we hit port?

Jenna did embark on adventures during port calls, despite our efforts to keep her on board for her own safety. Her only authorized time ashore was during daily walks, when she'd trot down the pier to explore a new world with her nose. Picture a young sailor in his Cracker Jack uniform, straight-backed with short hair, walking a foxy red dog. This was an unusual sight in any port district, causing people to stop in their tracks. Down the pier and through the port security gate, they'd pass worn warehouses and dilapidated shops in this transition zone from sea to land.

But to Jenna, it was a cauldron of exciting smells.

She would stop, resisting the pull of the leash while she snuffled an odiferous wind-borne stew of fish guts, fried noodles, and diesel fumes. Her sailor would stand patiently, in no hurry because he had duty and would not be hitting the town today. Jenna's nose painted a 4D-stratified catalog of what had occurred there over the past month. Eventually she would allow the walk to continue, traversing the half-industrial, half-commercial district at a slow pace. Most passersby were workers, intent on their tasks.

An elderly couple with a yellow sun umbrella stopped to offer their hands to Jenna, smiling but unable to speak English. Jenna approached and delicately sniffed their hands but backed away from being petted. The couple looked at one another and laughed, then the old man patted the young sailor on the shoulder as they parted.

The sailor extended their walk beyond the planned fifteen minutes, enjoying the new sights but also hoping to run into someone his age. Jenna was a proven chick magnet, which translated across any language barrier. They eventually retraced their steps, entering the port gate as colors sounded on the ship. The sailor stood at attention, saluting with his right hand while holding the leash with his left. Then it was back to the ship, where Jenna laid on the quarterdeck experiencing this exotic land through her exceptional nose until she hitched a rideshare with another sailor.

22.

DESPERATE MEASURES IN HONG KONG

I wish to have no Connection with any Ship
that does not Sail fast
for I intend to go in harm's way.

— CAPTAIN JOHN PAUL JONES

reen hills rose steeply from Victoria Harbor, towering above a monopoly of skyscrapers. Hong Kong was an intriguing blend of cutting-edge technology and ancient Chinese customs, of Western bars and tiny dim sum eateries, of garish neon-lit streets and peaceful parks, of obscenely rich businessmen living in luxury high rises overlooking a vast flotilla of derelict boats where families lived without basic human necessities.

We, the fortunate *Vandy* few, had to single-handedly suffer through all the port visits that had been booked for our departed Strike Group. Sniff. Hong Kong turned out to be an auspicious fortune not foretold by any cookie. As an added dividend, like finding a hundred-dollar bill after winning the lottery, we had the place all to ourselves. We would not have to contend with ten thousand sailors from the aircraft carrier and her escorts.

The final leg to our Triple Crown win was that we moored pierside at Kowloon, sharing the pier with a white cruise ship that dwarfed the *Vandy*. Pier space in Hong Kong was rare and expensive; I think we paid $8,000 per day, an extravagant price back then. Normally frigates moored to a buoy in Hong Kong harbor, and sailors took slow water taxis to and from shore. Mooring to a pier was a luxury reserved for the Admiral's flagship. (Did I mention he was en route to the Arabian Gulf?) I had been to Hong Kong half a dozen times but never moored pierside. This meant the crew could walk ashore rather than spending hours ferrying to and from the ship. It also meant that I didn't have to worry about the ship vacillating from a buoy, subject to winds, currents, and wayward ships. No chance of getting an anxious call about dragging anchor.

Hong Kong is a wonder of the world. More than just a beauty queen, it shared the title as a global financial center with New York and London. It had one of the largest per capita incomes but also the biggest income inequality among developed nations. Sixty-story buildings of glass and steel rivaled any in the world, yet workers swayed hundreds of feet above heavy traffic on bamboo scaffolding as they built the next skyscraper. China had taken control of Hong Kong from the British two years earlier, but I didn't notice anything different from my last visit. Yet. The change in ownership would be dramatically highlighted to *Vandy* and entire US Navy.

Anything was available here. *Anything.* Shopping was world renowned, whether one wanted to buy an authentic Chanel bag or a knockoff. There were huge shopping malls and too many shops, both famous and local, to count. Hong Kong tailors were well known for their fast and reliable workmanship, and generations of sailors bought their first suits here. Tailors' shills greeted sailors at the dock, displaying a list of previous Navy customers to steer business to their shops. Proprietors served cold beer and attended to patrons with care. Before they knew what hit them, sailors had ordered tailored suits, shirts, and a bunch of other clothes they hadn't known they needed—all to be delivered before leaving port in a few days, and for less than an off-the-rack suit from Macy's.

Dining and drinking were also world class. One hundred fifty-five years of British rule led to great Indian restaurants and pubs serving fresh Guinness on tap sprinkled throughout the city. Chinese food from any province was on every street, in any price range, for any taste. I found "real" Chinese food to be far different from our Americanized version. For the Chinese, the more fat the better. A chicken foot or two added some crunch. The mix of old and new extended to the pubs, which served cold draft beer or something more exotic.

On my first foray ashore, I stopped at a bar close to the pier. I was not stunned to find shipmates there experiencing the "culture." While enjoying an ice-cold Tsingtao beer, the specimens in jars above the bar caught my eye. I had seen similar displays of critter-liquor in Japan, the most famous being habu sake. Capturing a poisonous habu snake and plunging it into a large jar of sake wine so it strikes as it drowns made this the drink of choice for inebriated Japanese businessmen. When choosing this drink, one was "picking his poison." People paid twenty dollars (equivalent to thirty-five dollars today) a shot for this foul-smelling concoction in order to gain the strength of the habu, a potent snake that can go for an entire year without food.

In Hong Kong, they made similar drinks with multiple-headed snakes, scorpions, or other repugnant ingredients. But up on a shelf above the bar among the many clear bottles sat the crème de la crème of foul potions.

A mole fetus suspended in alcohol.

I couldn't imagine what powers might be passed on from this drink. Blind luck? An ability to dig where no human has dug before? This was just another way to see how far someone would take a dare. We all laughed... and drank...and talk grew bolder.

I offered fifty dollars to the fool who would drink a shot of that revolting concoction. I was not worried at all about having to take my wallet out; this was too disgusting for even hardened sailors. After lots of banter and bluster, and a few more beers, Petty Officer Craig Conrad stepped up to the plate. Craig's sonar technical acumen and leadership were primary reasons why we were able to sink the only sub during the RIMPAC exercise, but I started to reconsider his common sense.

The bartender stepped up on a chair and gingerly slid the large pickle jar to the edge of the shelf, took a deep breath, and lifted it. A cloud of dust blossomed, encapsulating the bartender. He sneezed and wavered. I was sure he was going to drop the jar, but he recovered and stepped down with the rotten prize. He wiped the top of the jar with a dingy bar towel and, with one arm encircling the barrel-like jar, twisted the cap with all his might. After a few minutes of wrestling, the lid released its aged grip. He slid the jar toward us and stepped back. Way back. The stench was immediate and overwhelming. We abandoned the counter and held our noses, squinting and gagging.

That fifty dollars was safe in my wallet.

The bartender fashioned a bandana from a bar towel and approached the jar. We could only see his eyes, which were squinted down to slits, and his bandana laying flaccid against his face. He poured a large shot and quickly twisted the top closed. We watched, entranced, unable to wrench our eyes away. The viscous light-brown liquid had drifting particles of something—mole?—that reflected the light like tiny fish scales. Somehow the smell had gotten worse, a sharp-biting-sickly smell like a skunk that had died under your house a week ago. Craig looked around, helpless, caught between bravado and common sense. This should have been fun for the rest of us, but the smell and spectacle were so disturbing that it took all my willpower not to retch.

Craig stepped forward, snatched up the shot glass, gulped the drink down, gagged, swallowed, and gagged again. We all gagged. He kept it down, drinking the rest of his beer in one swig while wildly motioning for another with his free hand.

Craig is still living today, but he did not leave Hong Kong unscathed. While wandering the streets, high on mole spirits, he was arrested and charged with rape. He was the main suspect, based on being apprehended in the woman's neighborhood and his inability to explain why he was there. Craig spent three weeks in a hotel, courtesy of the Hong Kong police, after we sailed away without him. He was eventually cleared by DNA tests.

As we prepared to depart Hong Kong, our recent close call with a freighter was on my mind. Hong Kong was (and still is) one of the busiest ports in the world, so we spent extra time preparing. Every kind of craft in the world operated here. The famous green ferries continuously crossed the channel between Hong Kong Island and Kowloon on mainland China. They had the right of way, and they flaunted it. Oil tankers, freighters, and other commercial ships transited day and night. Junks, sampans, fishing boats, and every variety of small boat were going somewhere, doing something. All were in a hurry, rushing in every direction and not planning to turn unless collision was imminent. Just keeping track of all these contacts took a focused and coordinated effort from the bridge and combat information center team. Evaluating which ones posed a threat to us was the final, critical step.

We cleared Victoria Harbor and reached the channel in one piece, safely headed to sea. Less traffic here, less chance of a problem, we breathed a collective sigh of relief.

We breathed too soon.

Two ships in formation appeared three miles ahead of us, cutting across our intended path from right to left. One was a warship, slightly smaller than *Vandy*, while the other was unmarked. We turned to starboard (right) to pass astern of them, the safest route to avoid them and stay in the channel. Both ships immediately turned 180 degrees, still in formation, to block our new path. We called them on the VHF bridge-to-bridge radio and asked their intentions. No reply. But we were prepared, even for this. Petty Officer Frank Yuan took the microphone and queried them in Mandarin. Three times.

Still no reply.

Great Britain had recently handed Hong Kong over to China, and there were questions about how things would be handled by the new regime. Would democracy be folded under the Communist wing, or would it survive?

Two miles now.

That's a long distance in a car, but a ship without brakes and constrained by a channel has limited options. They had my attention. I called for the Snoopy Team, a small posse of sailors who took pictures and recorded observations of other warships. We turned left, intending again to cut behind our two antagonists. We were at sea and anchor detail, so all stations were fully manned and both engines were on line. I called down to the engineering control room and told the Chief Engineer to ensure we were ready for quick maneuvering. Those drag races we had participated in were about to pay off.

The two ships—I never knew if they were acting on their own or under orders—turned again to cut us off.

This was a serious—and threatening—game of *chicken of the sea*.

I got down from my chair, rousing Jenna from her nap. She followed me out to the starboard bridge wing, neck stiff and ears at attention. She sensed the tension, probably smelling chemicals released from our pores and observing the increasing tempo. There was little talk, the silence broken only by a countdown of the distance to our antagonists. I crossed the bridge to the port wing, where I got a sense of the overall traffic and how much maneuvering room we had. Jenna followed at my heel, abandoning her favored side to discover the source of the static in the air. She couldn't see over the metal shielding where I stood, so she marched aft a few feet to look between the lifelines.

One mile and closing fast.

They were scanning us with binoculars from their bridges. What was their intent? I had to consider the risk of collision and possible damage, damage that could cost millions and take the ship off the front lines for many months. I had to consider the risk to the lives of my sailors.

I had to consider stopping the ship.

On the other hand, I had to weigh national pride and the message sent as a result of this test of our resolve and skill. These were no policemen, at least not ones we answered to. And I had a hidden advantage. I had authored the Navy's maritime interception tactics and helped execute UN sanctions against uncooperative Iraqi ships during Desert Shield. I knew how to blockade better than they did, and therefore how to beat them at their game. They had the advantage of being in their home waters, the element of surprise, and control of the choke point through which we must pass. We had speed and agility...and the next move. Time to show them what the US Navy could do.

Damn the torpedoes, full speed ahead!

"All Engines Ahead Flank!"

The bow surged, slicing the water into white foam on both sides.

"Right Hard Rudder!"

The *Vandy* heeled over as she turned. We flew past both ships, watching them turn to block us. Too late, too slow, SUVs against a Ferrari.

Jenna barked furiously at the Chinese ships as we passed, back arched and tail rigid rather than the normal rainbow curve. She expressed our indignation at their dangerous show and announced our defiance and superiority. Her war cries broke the tension, and everyone laughed as I picked her up and carried her inside. On to open waters, another story to tell.

China banned US Navy ships from visiting Hong Kong later that year to show us there was a new sheriff in town.

The Chinese Navy would soon test us again.

23.

JENNA SHANGHAIED

A good Navy is not a provocation to war.
It is the surest guaranty of peace.

—*President Theodore Roosevelt*

Shanghai. The name conjures images of Far Eastern intrigue, long painted nails tapping on lacquer boxes, smoky opium dens, and dangerous bars filled with wharf riffraff—riffraff in danger of being *shanghaied*, forced to serve on ships against their will. By far the biggest city in the world, Shanghai had more than twice the population of New York City. An ancient city more than twelve hundred years old, it was industrial, hectic, money-driven and yet impoverished by our standards. Shanghai had seen war and decades of occupation by the British and Japanese. General Vandegrift served there in 1927–28, for which he received the Yangtze Service Medal. This wouldn't be the last time we followed in the General's large footsteps.

Few US sailors had ever visited this mysterious, exotic, and forbidden port. We were chosen to *show the flag* in Shanghai—to wave it proudly in China in order to make an imprint of the US Navy's warfighting readiness, while at the same time extending a hand in friendship. Despite our recent showdown in Hong Kong and the subsequent ban on Navy ship visits to that city-state, there was a desire to improve relations with the People's Republic of China (PRC). Military-to-military engagement was an important part of building mutual confidence. Admiral Joseph Prueher, the four-star Commander in Chief of Pacific forces, had visited Shanghai a month ago for high-level discussions. We were the second course. I wondered if they had chosen us because of our recent dustup in Hong Kong or in spite of it.

Rear Admiral Harry Highfill, commander of amphibious forces in the Western Pacific, embarked aboard *Vandy* for this groundbreaking visit. He was an aviator who had served only on bigger, lumbering amphibious ships. It was always challenging to host an Admiral on board, like your boss's boss staying at your house for a week.

There was one other small package on board that was new to him. Jenna met the Admiral when he stepped into the wardroom for his first meal. Admiral Highfill was a big man, one of those football players who retained his mass but whose outline had softened. His aide, Lieutenant John Fuller, was just as big with a younger cut. Together they filled some serious space on our trim ship. The officers waiting for lunch were acting casual, doing everything but whistling tunelessly with eyes to the heavens. The Admiral stepped in, grinning and shaking hands. His hands were like big mitts, well worn but soft and enveloping. As he turned left to greet those near the TV, he stopped short when he spotted Jenna sitting upright on the couch returning his gaze. His smile unfroze an instant later, and he continued his meet and greet. When he got to Jenna, he gave her a soft pat, which Jenna received as graciously as she could. In other words, she sat still.

As the Admiral ordered lunch, he turned to me with a crooked smile.

"That was a surprise. I haven't seen a dog on board a ship."

"That's Jenna." I attempted a nonchalant smile. "She's our mascot."

The table was silent, everyone focused on our conversation. Sort of like the old EF Hutton commercials when everything stood still.

"How great! I wasn't aware that ships had mascots like that anymore."

"Well...most don't." My voice trailed off. "In fact, we might be the only one."

His grin grew full as he gave me a thumbs-up.

The silent spell was broken as officers returned to their meals and conversations. The Admiral immediately became an honorary *Vandy* shipmate rather than a senior officer that required attention. His aide proved just as affable and would go on to become a well-respected Admiral.

The transit up the Yangtze River was long and chaotic. Shanghai was the second busiest commercial port in the world and would take that crown from Singapore in 2010. We hoisted a PRC flag, the symbol of one of the US's global challengers, up the mast as two Chinese pilots embarked.

There was immediate consternation.

The US Naval Attaché explained that our huge American "battle flag" was dwarfing the small red PRC flag. Apparently *size matters* in flags. Straining to act diplomatically, we downsized to match their flag. We soon rendezvoused with the *Anqing*, a brand-new PRC frigate brought in from another port. We were once again comparing size and strength, flexing biceps in front of one other. *Vandy* was to follow *Anqing* into port, a four-hour trip up the Yangtze.

The traffic scheme was reversed here, so we had to drive on the left side of the channel. This was expected and by itself not difficult. But the overwhelming volume of traffic, like rush hour in Los Angeles except at full speed, did not heed *any* rules of the road. It was chaos as ships rushed in all directions, disregarding navigational rules or even common sense. To make matters worse, our escort took off up the channel at twenty knots, weaving between tankers and freighters in a crazy game of chicken.

What to do?

Remain at a safe twelve knots and pick our way through?

No, this was another test of national will and nerve.

We came up to speed, maneuvering among the crowded throng. (I am wincing as I write this; thank goodness it went well.) To add to the fun, both pilots were yammering directions and getting increasingly upset because no one was paying attention to them.

As we navigated upstream against the tide of merchants, we also took notes for the Fleet Commander. Admiral Blacker. Even three-star Admirals look for good liberty. The Seventh Fleet commander wanted to visit Shanghai if the USS *Blue Ridge*, his flagship, could fit into port. We were recording water depths, channel width, and bridge clearances that were not listed on charts. Our survey information must have been accurate; *Blue Ridge* would later follow our trail without running aground or striking a bridge. If we had an incident, however slight, I am sure Admiral Blacker already had someone lined up to replace me.

Our visit to Shanghai was important for the US and China. Both were playing a game of chess to expand power and influence in the Western Pacific. The US remained the big dog, even in that faraway neighborhood, but China was improving their fleet, and this was a home game for them. As we approached the pier, we saw a full band and sailors in formation. We were not using tugs, as usual, but went in using our own power.

I took quick glances as I stood high on the bridge wing, measuring the gap between the *Anqing* moored ahead of us and a merchant parked astern. I had enough space to parallel park but had to consider the current and wind, as well as how those factors would change once we got closer to the pier.

Vandy had just one screw (propeller), which rotated counterclockwise when viewed from astern of the ship and thereby pushed the stern to starboard. This could be challenging, but we had a hidden device. Actually, two of them. They were auxiliary propulsion units (APUs), which were small, trainable screws mounted on either side of the bow. We could parallel park the ship into tight spaces without the help of tugs or pilots. I wanted our landing to look professional and sharp, no seesawing back and forth to get lined up on the mark. We didn't just have to fit into our space but also needed to be aligned to hook up the brow, electrical cables, sewer, and water services.

We drove in at five knots. That does not sound fast, but try parallel parking your car at six miles per hour without using the brakes. We used the APUs to quickly decelerate, simultaneously pushing the ship toward the pier. The boatswain's mates heaved monkey fists, heavy knots resembling fists that were attached to light lines. Sailors ashore caught them and pulled the attached mooring lines to the pier, securing them to bollards. We were tied up in ten minutes, which was quick for a ship. I have seen cars take longer trying to parallel park.

First impression made.

The Admiral and I went ashore to greet our welcoming committee, trading salutes, shaking hands, and exchanging short, translated courtesies. As I shook the Chinese General's hand, I noticed that his eyes were fixed over my shoulder. I glanced back and saw Jenna's head protruding from between the lifelines as she took in the sights and smells of this new port. The wind was blowing the tendrils of her blondish tail, her own gently waving stalk of grain. He returned his gaze to me, a questioning look but no words. I smiled and shrugged my shoulders, and his cheeks rose into a wide smile.

The first genuine smile of the afternoon.

We were immersed over the next few days in a cavalcade of banquets, tours, and sporting events designed to build camaraderie with our naval counterparts. We were not tasked to gather intelligence, though we provided feedback on this visit like we did after every port call. I was surprised to discover how much the Chinese junior officers knew about *Vandy* and to hear their detailed questions. No doubt they had been tasked with gathering information.

We toured the brand-new *Anqing*, the pride of the growing Chinese fleet. It was less impressive inside than out, a generation behind my fourteen-year-old ship. Although we only got a cursory look, their weapons systems and electronics looked far less sophisticated than ours. I perceived little ability to withstand a hit; the ship had many flammables and limited damage control equipment. It was eye-opening. I would not take them for granted in battle, knowing that the quality of the captain and crew were as meaningful as their ship's hardware. But their technology was far below what Western navies considered modern.

Shanghai images pass through the viewfinder in my head to this day. This enormous city expanded from the river in every direction, overlooked by the Oriental Pearl Tower. That impressive structure, which sat across the river from the ship, had eleven balls of decreasing size. It was colorful by day and dazzling by night, a Chinese Eiffel Tower. The city was an intriguing mix of ancient China and Western modernity, millions of poor living in squalid conditions not far from one of the richest trade centers in the world.

Shanghai was one of the most populous cities in the world. Lots of people, lots of traffic, but little color. The streets were packed with trucks and dull-colored Jettas. It seemed every car was a Jetta, an eccentricity worthy of a *Seinfeld* episode. They manufactured Jettas here, and every one of them was a drab color. Perhaps it was not wise to be ostentatious in a Communist country. This huge municipality was spread across more than twenty-four hundred square miles, all of it drab gray and beige matching the smog. Embedded like gems in a sandbox were a handful of colorful, shining temples with large, manicured gardens.

There were still many things marked "Made in China." Although most items available here were cheap trinkets, there were a few high-end retail shops for the city's elite. Beanie Babies were manufactured here, so these stuffed toys were sold in every store and at every roadside stand. They were a hot commodity back home, traded like stocks. Even the rare ones were available here, supposedly worth hundreds of dollars. Because we couldn't afford a Ming vase or Fendi handbag, we bought a Beanie Baby or two as future presents. Some of those Babies never made it home. For months I found Jenna carrying a different Beanie Baby around the ship, treasuring it for a few days until she became bored.

We briefed the crew that there might be attempts to draw information from them, mainly by soft means. That meant they wouldn't be tied up and water-boarded, but agents might try nonaggressive methods. A red flag should go up if someone was too friendly, especially a beautiful woman. If it seemed too good to be true, it probably was too good to be true. We also recommended care when exploring this enormous city since we had no idea where the "bad" neighborhoods were.

The Hard Rock Café became one of the crew hangouts, familiar yet packed with locals. Black crew members were an anomaly and treated like stars, reporting that locals asked if they were Michael Jackson or Boyz II Men. Of course, the guys played along if the inquirer was female. Even at the Hard Rock the crew ran into a language barrier when a server did not understand an order for Peking duck. After much quacking and arm flapping, the waitress laughed and indicated they didn't serve it.

I found out later, much later, that the crew frequented an indoor go-kart raceway. The ad that got their attention:

"Go-karts and a bar. Together. Under one roof. Open until 2 a.m. Drinking and driving is not discouraged—in fact, it's expected."

That sounded as close to heaven as they expected to get, and it was all under one roof. Somehow everyone survived with all their fingers and toes.

The best thing that we did for the crew was to arrange and help fund tours to Beijing. Many took the eight-hundred-mile trip to the Great Wall and toured the capital city. Despite heavy snow, every one of them raved about walking on one of the Seven Wonders of the World. The crew wanted to take Jenna with them, but the risk was too high. She had to stay behind with me and take care of the ship.

The Chinese Navy challenged us to a soccer game. The invitation specifically invited "the dog" to come along. I smiled when I read that part—the general had visibly warmed when he spied Jenna during our arrival. When the bus arrived, Jenna was waiting with everyone else. I had the dog watch, since I was not playing. I wish I could say that we let them win for international diplomacy, but they just kicked our butts. Soccer was unappreciated in the US at this time, so we had few players with any experience.

Jenna sat quietly on the sidelines, disinterested in the game, swiveling her head based on something smelled or heard. At one point the action came to our feet, and she pulled on the leash to chase the players as they ran past. After the game the competitors lined up and shook hands. As I walked Jenna through the line, each player grinned and asked permission, by hand signal and raised eyebrows, to pet her. A group photograph, with Jenna smack in front, was taken. The interpreter told me the General planned to put the picture in the newspaper and even planned to send it to higher headquarters with his report. I managed a weak smile.

As the bus wove its way back to the pier, the smile slipped off my face. I hoped that a photograph in a Chinese city newspaper, even one as significant as Shanghai's, would never make it back to US eyes.

Admiral Blacker's face flashed in my mind.

I absently stroked Jenna as I gazed out the window, absorbing nothing as my mind twirled.

Getting underway from a good port visit is like hitting the sack after a long night of partying. We don't want the fun to end but are spent and relieved to be getting back to a routine. Our visit to Shanghai was a step forward in Sino-American relations and provided a glimpse into the vast empire and richness of China. This country dwarfed ours in terms of history, culture, size, and population. Chinese leadership views geopolitics and strategy in terms of centuries rather than the hurried, react-to-the-twenty-four-hour-news-cycle we are driven by. Of course, there are scores of attributes—freedom, human rights, innovation, liberal education—in which we are head and shoulders above China. Traveling imparts a sense of the broader global picture—things are done differently, not necessarily incorrectly, in other countries. It made each of us appreciate that we lived in the best country in the world—a country that would fight for the freedom of others on every sea.

We set the sea and anchor detail, ready to make our way back through the Christmas-like rush of vessels. I had made sure the team got back on board at a decent hour the night before, so everyone was lucid for another challenging sea detail. As we prepared to shift our colors, Rhino asked which American flag he should haul up alongside the PRC flag. He was holding the folded battle ensign (US flag), the one that covered most of the mast and would dwarf the PRC flag. He stood there expectantly, resembling Jenna when she knows you have a treat. I gave him a thumbs-up. He grinned ear to ear and quick-marched to the mast.

I was not trying to make China look bad. On the contrary, I felt we had made friends and built some trust during this visit. But we could not appear timid. I wanted our rivals to recognize that the US Navy was proud and combat ready. That should they contemplate entering into a conflict with us, they must consider the bold warfighters they would face. We went big and went home!

24.

BABY KONG

*Sailors have the cleanest bodies
and the filthiest minds.*

— ELEANOR ROOSEVELT

A sailor's eyes will glaze over and a silly-sly grin emerge if you mention Thailand. Not even a spousal jab to the solar plexus can bring him fully back to the present. Anyone who has visited this exotic land can close their eyes and see colorful, teeming street markets and serrated golden temples. Can smell the curry-basil-pepper aroma that permeates the air. Can feel the wavelets washing fine sand over their feet as they gaze at a string of vibrant green Stonehenge rocks just offshore. Can hear the constant hawking of peddlers...and the laughter of a people who always find something to smile at. And can see the women who are renowned for their beauty.

Our port visit to Pattaya Beach was much less political, and much more raucous, than Shanghai. Of all the ports in the Western Pacific, the most over-the-top sea stories came from Thailand. Wives flew in to spend time with their husbands in ports we visited...but not to Thailand. It was an unwritten rule that spouses were not brought to this party. Pattaya Beach is at the country's geographical crotch, Thailand's right leg spread wide to Malaysia with a Singapore-toe, the left knee bent at Cambodia with a foot resting against Vietnam (see the chart on page 11).

Soldiers of many countries have waged war in the jungles here, and navies have battled pirates in these humid seas for hundreds of years. With war came strife, hardship, and poverty. People did what was necessary to survive, and still do. Thais somehow came through it with wide smiles and an indelible sense of humor, appreciating today's sun rather than worrying about yesterday's cloudburst. They lead simple lives in a paradise of blue water and sandy beaches, the ocean providing an incredible bounty of lobsters, jumbo shrimp, and fish.

And occasionally delivering a ship full of sailors with money burning holes in their dungarees.

We were here as part of Cobra Gold, an annual exercise to strengthen US ties with Thailand, a friendly and strategically positioned country. Thailand was one of the few Southeast Asian countries to support the United States during the Vietnam War. We had a few days ashore to coordinate with our Thai Navy counterparts before starting this two-week exercise. A few days to plan...a few nights to explore this famed haunt.

We anchored offshore as there was no pier large enough for the *Vandegrift*. The voyage to shore was a maritime version of planes, trains, and automobiles. First, we climbed down our accommodation ladder and into a water taxi that held twenty people. The rub came as we approached shore. There was no pier on which to drop us off, so our water taxi had to stop a hundred yards offshore as the water became shallow. A fifteen-foot narrow wooden boat sidled alongside the water taxi, and ten of us climbed down onto the lurching craft and sat on wooden benches that ran perpendicular to the boat, much like pews.

The boat, like the others lined up to ferry follow-on passengers, was well worn. It had a distinctive prow that extended a few feet beyond the bow, arching toward the sky in a graceful curve. Running rust from sea-worn bolts stained the boat's faded white sides with orange tiger stripes at one-foot intervals. The captain (who was also the entire crew) stood in the back under a thatch umbrella, wielding a wooden handle attached to a small motor that was attached to an eight-foot shaft that ended at the propeller. He steered by pulling the handle, and thus the entire contraption, right or left. We hit the beach at full speed, running up onto the sand. We took off our shoes and hopped over the side into the water, trudging a few feet ashore.

After seeing all the moving, wet parts of getting ashore, it was clear that Jenna had to stay on board the ship. I was relieved. I had been wondering how she would do in this Wild West setting and worried that we would never find her if she got lost. The convoluted transfer ashore, even more hazardous at night, made my decision easy. But it was not well received by everyone.

Jenna hung out on the quarterdeck each day, finding a spot shaded from the savage sun. She watched her shipmates take off full of vim and vigor in the morning and return at night needing help to make it up the ladder and into their racks. Although she looked over the side to watch sailors jump onto the lively water taxi, she never tried to venture down the steep ladder to the choppy water's edge. In between boat arrivals she gazed toward the town a few miles away, nose elevated and quivering. Could she smell Thai basil, coriander, and lemongrass? Or was the air too tainted with the stale bouquet of Singha beer and cheap perfume emanating from her returning shipmates?

Pattaya Beach was built around a magnificent white sand beach. The main street followed the slow curve of the coast, each side crowded with restaurants, bars, gem stores, bars, hotels, and more bars. Did I mention there was a party going on?

Twenty-four seven.

The revelry heated up as the tropical sun lost its punch and lights strung from palm trees blinked on. After dinner many of the largest restaurants turned into...bars. I watched waiters in one establishment move tables and chairs, setting up a kickboxing ring where diners had sat minutes before. Blood and teeth were spilled as blank-faced boxers, high on something, kicked the living shit out of each other for a dollar or two. After a few bouts between local fighters, a red-faced sailor stood up and stripped off his shirt. His buddies cheered, thumping him on the back when he passed. As he stumbled down the stairs, his face showed hesitation, belatedly wondering whether this was a good idea. But his pride, goaded on by his shipmates' hoots, drove him into the ring. I was glad that he was not one of my sailors.

They taped on his gloves, and he stumbled into the ring through the grimy ropes. The Muay Thai boxer looked on with a blank face. This was just another day at the office, and he was ready to show off his street boxing skills for a few baht (Thai currency). The flushed sailor came out swinging, missing roundhouses until a foot to his stomach stopped him cold. He took a few more punches to the head before he was able to grapple with the smaller local. After the referee split them apart, it was a minute or two until the sailor gave up, bruised and bloody, not yet feeling the pain that would hit hard after the alcohol wore off. A loser in the ring but a champion among his shipmates.

Sailors dream in fifty shades of red light. Thai resort towns were set up to extract money from foreign visitors. Like any good businesspeople—and Thais were shrewd—they offered what customers wanted. And at the top of many young men's lists is sex, which has always been one of the greatest temptations. Thailand was one of the sex capitals of the world. European men have *vacationed* here for a century, and American and Australian tourists have now joined them. Thai girls were beautiful, dubbed the most attractive in the Far East or even in the entire world. In Thailand even the males were beautiful. No, I didn't swing like that, but these *lady-boys* were such adept cross-dressers that they were easily mistaken for women. Sailors learned to take a hard look for telltale signs: a slight Adam's apple, shoulders a bit too wide, hands or feet larger than a girl's, or a raspy or deeper voice.

Sex was cheap and available. In fact, it smacked you in the face. The working girls were omnipresent and aggressive; one had to adamantly say no and keep saying it. As I walked down the street, I avoided making eye contact to avoid aggressive sales pitches. But the "bar girls," a nice name for the prostitutes, good-naturedly traded barbs and shared lychee once they determined that I was not interested in their trade. Thais had an incredible sense of humor, always ready to laugh at or with you. Smiles were the norm, even though most lived in near poverty.

Not all the working women walked the streets. The more formal establishments had muted lighting and small tables with brass chairs well-spaced for privacy, all oriented toward a bright, glassed-in lounge. Twenty or so women sat on carpeted steps or meandered about the small inner lounge dressed in formal gowns, lipstick and makeup perfect, each with a number affixed to her clothing. A barman read off a number, and the woman with that number made her way out of the neon cage to sit with the person who had expressed interest in her. If she made the right impression, they went upstairs on a "date." If not, back to the glass cage. Some of the numbers indicated a certain skill or proclivity.

We were oblivious to human trafficking in the '90s, ignorant of the huge trade that forces women and girls into prostitution. I don't know how much of what we saw was voluntary and how much was forced—if not forced by criminals, at least forced by poverty. What seemed to be a good time then, even mutually beneficial, now seems improper.

Pattaya Beach and Phuket were playgrounds for foreign tourists. Although a third-world country, Thailand's main tourist areas were well kept and focused on keeping visitors happy. However, there was much more to this exotic and complicated country than these tourist resorts. I took a day trip to visit Thailand's most renowned city to see if "One Night in Bangkok" would make the world my oyster. Bangkok was the geographic, political, and cultural center of Thailand, with a population comparable to New York City.

Upon arrival at this congested capital, I was first struck by the traffic. In fact, I was nearly physically struck by the traffic several times. It seemed that all eight million residents were riding some sort of motorized vehicle, usually a motorbike, with all their possessions piled high on the back. Each appeared late for an important rendezvous—it looked like motorized mixed martial arts at high speed. Horns blared, engines revved, and cycles dashed between mini-trucks and cars, jockeying to save a few seconds at risk to life and limb. Small children clung to their drivers like baby monkeys, without helmets or fear.

The smog was impermeable and palpable. Not the light-brown haze that hangs over Los Angeles, this polluted atmosphere was personal and compacted down to eye level. I smelled diesel mixed with rancid cooking oil, with an occasional whiff of spices. At thirteen degrees latitude, Bangkok was much closer to the equator than Key West or even Honolulu. The average temperature was ninety-two degrees, but it was much hotter during the summer. This was monsoon country, which meant it rained like a mother-father. Sixty-five inches of annual rainfall ensured there was plenty of moisture to mix with the heat, forming a barrier of humidity that I had to swim against in the crowded streets. It was like a soggy ole dog blanket hanging heavy and dripping on my shoulders, ripe with odors.

The compressed atmosphere was exacerbated by the crowd density. I thought I had seen big throngs. St Patrick's Day in New York City, Easter Sunday at the Vatican, Friday night in Tokyo...Shanghai, Karachi, Moscow, Los Angeles. The semi-annual shoe sale at Nordstrom Rack. Not one of those compared to the sardine-can conditions in Bangkok.

So beside the crowds, how was the play? Bangkok was an amazing city where you could find the full range of food. Thai food has always been my favorite, but like most ethnic foods it has been tempered in the US to appeal to American palates. The spices here were the same, just toned down so our tongues didn't burn off. Bangkok had the most incredible seafood restaurants, serving a mind-blowing array of fresh and live seafood. I went to one that comfortably seated more than a thousand people.

Then there was the other end of the spectrum in the smaller establishments. I consumed proteins that were not beef or chicken, despite what the menu said. The texture and smell were distinctly different. I told myself that my meal was a thin water buffalo, not a stringy cat. In the mood for a cricket? There were many varieties served in street stalls. Grasshoppers fried for crunch or caterpillars left alive to preserve their juicy texture—it was all there. I won't detail the caged animals at the market, but what we consider forbidden—*woof, woof*—was available in every color and shape. Jenna would have been appalled.

On our final night in Pattaya Beach I strolled down the main street that was closed to cars for the evening but jammed with people, bicycles, and small motorbikes. Hawkers accosted me every few feet. Thailand was famous for rubies and sapphires and had become a worldwide center for mining, trading, and processing gems. One gentleman on the street proved that his large stone was a sapphire by cutting glass with it. Although impressed, I was able to resist that scam. Gems, genuine and false, were everywhere. It was difficult to distinguish the imposters—a bogus gem had no Adam's apple.

As I headed back to the ship, I heard loud chattering and spotted a monkey held above the crowd and heading directly toward me. It turned out to be Dave Richardson (my new navigator), Matt LaPointe, and Nate Johnston. Matt had a small monkey hanging onto his neck, which he brought down for me to see. These nuts had bought a monkey...and Matt didn't even drink. Even worse, they wanted to bring the newly named Baby Kong on board the ship as another mascot. I had visions of the monkey running and swinging wildly around the ship, shitting everywhere, turning switches, pushing buttons, pulling apart fixtures, opening valves, and getting into food.

Torturing Jenna.

Nightmare. Despite having a few drinks under my belt, it was a quick and easy decision.

No! There could be only one mascot. We were not running a zoo.

The monkey never made the trip to our anchored ship.

Thailand, a country of absolutes.

Beauty. Smog. Humor. Hunger. Sex. Food. Jewels. Silk.

Small wonder this place of dreams enticed so many sailors to go AWOL.

25.

SHELLBACKS AND WOGS

I'm glad I was in the Navy.

— YOGI BERRA

Two-thirds of the world is covered by ocean, which the navy patrols every hour of every day. Patrols them night and day, in any conditions. Patrols enormous, empty swaths of water v-e-r-y s-l-o-w-l-y. That twelve-hour airline flight to Japan seems endless, despite flying at six hundred miles per hour. *Vandy* transited at twelve knots—about fourteen miles per hour—which meant our voyage from San Diego to Japan took three weeks. A twelve-hour flight doesn't seem so bad when compared to a five-hundred-hour transit. Our travel time did not include the necessary stopovers for fuel or severe weather delays. The strength of the Navy is its ability to deploy anywhere, just not instantly.

My navigator was Dave Richardson, who went on to command the destroyer USS *Porter*. You just met him in Thailand, right after he joined the ship. Dave had one tour under his belt, so he was no longer *cherry* (virginal, i.e., a new guy) but also not dripping with salt from years at sea. He became the leader of the junior officers (JOs) through his charisma and professional skills—and his penchant for having a great time anywhere, anytime. He and his quartermasters, the enlisted navigation experts, plotted *Vandy*'s route. Since the world is round, we couldn't draw a straight line on a flat chart that represented two dimensions of our curved, three-dimensional world. We could have, but it would have been like driving from Seattle to Boston via Dallas. They plotted courses on rhumb lines that took the earth's curvature into account.

Among all these lines running up (longitudes) and around (latitudes) the earth, some are special to those of us who sail past them. One can become a Blue Nose by crossing the Arctic Circle at 66 degrees, 32 minutes north latitude. That is north of Iceland, above even Nome. If someone is that far north, I imagine *any* exposed body part turns blue. *Vandy* had never gone that far north nor had I, so I can't tell you about it.

Ships cross the international date line any time they transit between the West Coast and the Western Pacific (WESTPAC). The mention of WESTPAC brings faraway looks and smiles of remembrance to sailors who reveled in the Wild West atmosphere in the Far East setting. The prime meridian of the world runs through the original site of the Royal Observatory at Greenwich, England, at

NEAL J. KUSUMOTO, CAPTAIN, US NAVY (RET)

longitude o degrees; every place on Earth is measured in terms of its distance east or west from this line. The international date line is in the middle of the Pacific, halfway around the globe from Greenwich along the 180th meridian.

There is no certificate for crossing the date line, but the date does change as the ship passes this imaginary line. Sailors, cynical by nature, believed that we timed our transits to skip Sundays (the day we held holiday routine while at sea) on the westward transit. Sometimes we skipped a day that fell on someone's birthday. Of course, that poor fellow lamented that he had thought the Navy could take away everything *except* his birthday.

The king of all lines is the equator. One joins the proud ranks of trusty Shellbacks upon crossing it—until then you are a slimy Pollywog (Wog). Our day of crossing was a full day, as in a twenty-four-hour day of fun. Fun for the Shellbacks, anyway. In fact, preparations had begun before leaving port, as Shellbacks acquired pirate clothing and Wogs obtained outfits for a talent show. Tensions rose as we approached the equator, the Shellbacks providing graphic details of what was about to befall the lowly Wogs. The bad news for the Wogs was that most of it came true. Shellbacks, who as the senior sailors were in positions of control, built their props and secretly started saving garbage a week before the ceremony. That garbage simmered and stewed in a secret location, ripening for the ceremony.

The traditional talent show was held on the evening before crossing. It was run like *The Gong Show*; Wogs performed acts until the audience bonged a large pot indicating they were bored or disgusted. We were cruising across a placid sea, dolphins and flying fish our only neighbors for hundreds of miles, with just the low rhythmic hum of the engines, the swish-hiss of water against the hull, and a slight breeze generated by our own headway. The crew stood on the flight deck in a semicircle, dressed in dungarees with white T-shirts. The sellout crowd murmured and shuffled, waiting for the curtain to rise. I was in the front row with Jenna, who was on a leash. She alternated sitting and standing, each time looking up at me trying to transmit an unambiguous message: *Let me go!* I held my ground—and her leash—concerned that this crowd might inadvertently trample her.

The first performance involved five young "women" dressed in assorted negligées with matching black steel-toed boots. They stood in a line laughing nervously while waiting for the music to start, eyeing the crowd, acknowledging the crude banter, and sending unladylike retorts back. "Candy Licker" by Marvin Sease began, a strip-club favorite. Not familiar with this classic? I pause here so you can listen to it on your mobile device as you read. If you have an impressionable child within earshot, you might want to put on earphones.

The "ladies" started their bump-and-grind routines, using their tongues to suggestively lick lollipops.

We exploded in laughter. The act brought us full circle...hard-core sailors pantomiming women who acted out what men wanted to see. As the crowd got into it, the performers gained courage and increased the heat, bringing up shipmates for audience participation. No one was about to gong this act, but the "ladies" finally tired and trudged off stage—it was hard to be elegant in work boots—to catcalls and applause.

That act would be hard to beat. The crowd good-naturedly gonged groups who had not gotten their act together or had feeble costumes. I noted that some of these "girls" looked disturbingly good...had they gotten tips during our Thailand visit? And where did they get all that feminine clothing? I decided this fit under the new "don't ask, don't tell" rule.

Imagine young sailors dressed in a wide range of cast-off women's clothing. Some were stout, some teenager thin, and some sported thick muscles with tattoos. Each performed their sexiest and most alluring dance moves, rendering in his mind's eye some amalgamation of a sexy girl at a high school dance and a stripper on stage. Thank goodness this was before cell phones with cameras.

Talent shows have since been emasculated by the Navy to ensure we maintain the *right spirit*, especially with mixed-sex crews. That rule is proper, but these shows were one of the most fun and memorable occasions at sea.

The pack roared when each act came out, straining to recognize the performers, chattering, laughing, hooting, and catcalling. The energy was electric, like that of a rock concert except more personal. We were sharing this together, adding tensile strength to already strong bonds, creating memories from performances at odds with our deadly mission.

Finally, only one group remained.

The crowd groaned as "YMCA" by the Village People started, the group popular with the gay disco community not being a crew favorite. We exchanged glances, wondering what mischief was at hand. And then there they were, marching to the beat. First out was the construction worker in a sleeveless plaid shirt, blue plastic helmet, and mustache. Next was the biker, a dark vest highlighting his bushy chest hair, tattoos and gold chains, a braided scarf as a headband, and mustache encircling his mouth then dripping into a goatee. The Indian wore a small braided headband, shirtless to show off the war paint on his chest and cheeks. The final member had on a blue dungaree shirt folded up to his chest showing his abs, sleeves rolled up to his shoulders, white Dixie cup at a rakish angle offsetting his black sunglasses. Last but not least, the sailor.

Our very own Village People, and they were on fire! I could barely hear the music blasting from nearby speakers because of the hysterical laughter and shouting. Their arms forming Ys may have been imperfect and out of synch, and they might have missed a character or two, but the crowd was eating it up. Dressing like women was funny. Dressing like gay men was one incongruous step further along the road to hilarity.

The song ended and the crowd groaned.

But wait, they were still posturing, waiting. For what?

They had an encore! I picked up Jenna as we approached rock concert madness. She struggled but quickly settled down as she realized that she could see what was happening from this height.

"In the Navy" blasted out. I thought we were at a fever pitch before, but the crowd reverberations were now strong enough to be tracked on sonar. Everyone was singing, jumping, laughing, and pointing. All else was forgotten, no thoughts of the next watch, personal problems, or even the many months remaining until we returned home.

It was one of those rare instances of pure joy, somehow transpiring in the middle of the Pacific Ocean as we neared the earth's equator.

Why did the performers work so hard on their acts and put up with the abuse? The winner got to sit beside King Neptune the next day, bypassing the "fun." King Neptune, as the Shellback who crossed the line before anyone else on board (in this case twenty years earlier), was in charge of the proceedings. He had sent me a formal dispatch proclaiming his intent to board and conduct the ceremony.

The talent show was the launch point of eighteen hours of mayhem. Firefights broke out on the night before the big day, Shellbacks getting an early start and Wogs taking preemptive shots. Chris Mirabella was a junior seaman but a born leader. He was smart enough to be the CEO of Facebook but possessed a gene that led him to trouble—Jenna and I visited him a few times after captain's masts. Chris found the chiefs' stashed garbage incubator and dumped some of it overboard before he was caught. He paid the price for this grievous transgression but was a hero to his fellow Wogs.

The day of crossing started early. I'm not sure of the exact time because my cabin was isolated high above the fray. Jenna and I slept until 4:00 a.m. when the din rose to our level. A band of the most rambunctious Wogs, the self-named *Vandy* Boyz, provided a special reveille. They were tarred and feathered—doused with honey and then dusted with feathers from old pillows—to become the Reveille Roosters. They made the rounds about the ship, visiting each berthing area while flapping their arms, stamping their feet, and crowing, "any-cock'l-do," rather than the prescribed "cock-a-doodle-do." At 4:00 a.m. this was not amusing or funny. The Roosters were run out of every area, *fowl* words echoing in their ears.

For twelve hours, Wogs travelled on hands and knees, at the mercy of the mighty Shellbacks. It was painful to crawl on a deck covered with non-skid, a coating grittier than sandpaper. Non-skid is intentionally rough to help sailors maintain their footing when the deck is wet and the ship is rolling. It was good for balance but punishing on palms and knees. Most Wogs wore knee and hand pads made from whatever materials they could find. Some added padding to the seat of their pants.

Wogs were eventually herded like sheep onto the forecastle, where there was no cover, and then sprayed with fire hoses. We were at 0 degrees latitude, so the predawn wind was chilly but not hazardous. Shellbacks, dressed like extras from *Pirates of the Caribbean*, had three-foot lengths of heavy fire hose in lieu of swords. They swung these shillelaghs, threatening the Wogs and paddling them on the butt. In years past it had been OK to wallop Wogs until they were black and blue. Closet sadists or others bent on revenge took their frustrations out on shipmates, and appropriate temperance had been applied. Now, it was done with less force, nothing hard enough to cause bruising. This was just a warm-up; the sun had not even risen. Those of us on the bridge watched an endless stream of dripping Wogs crawl past with their heads down enduring an age-old ritual marking their entrance into the club of ancient mariners.

Jenna was a Wog.

She too had to go through the ceremony. Of course, she was not on her knees—even if she could have, she wouldn't have—but was gingerly avoiding puddles as she checked out this insanity. Jenna walked among the huddled mass of shivering Wogs, looking intently at this strange behavior. By now she knew how things worked on the ship, and this was not normal. She avoided the fire hose area, preferring to remain clean and dry. Of course, no one dared raise a shillelagh in her direction.

After a long day of torture, the final act was held in the helicopter hanger. Last night this had been the scene of the raucous *Gong Show*, but today it had been transformed into a chamber of horrors. This was the last and most challenging series of entrance tests. The smell of rotting food was overpowering, even from a distance and in the open air. Wogs had to crawl through long plastic tunnels of rotting waste, squishing on hands and knees through unrecognizable filth. Mirabella might have dumped some of the garbage, but that didn't put a dent in this rancid cesspool. Many threw up along the way, their hot vomit adding a new dimension to the putrid passageway.

The worst part was the anticipation. Waiting in a long line, on hands and knees, hearing the retching and coughing, all of it blown out of proportion by the surrounding Shellbacks. After exiting the tunnel, each Wog kissed the blubbery, greased belly of the Royal Baby and then sucked a slippery garbanzo bean from his belly button and swallowed it. Next, the Royal Doctor, in a witch doctor costume that included a strand of chicken bones, injected a stream of fiery unidentifiable liquid into each mouth. The Royal Barber then dipped his wooden razor into a vat of fluorescent dyes and "cut" each Wog's hair until it glowed a bright color. Good thing we would be at sea for a while!

Only one Wog was unfazed. Jenna daintily sniffed along the edges of the scum pond but was banned after she was caught sampling the garbage. She found a dry place at the tunnel entrance and lay watching her fellow Wogs crawl by.

King Neptune and his court reviewed each Wog, then declared them Shellbacks.

We crossed the equator on May 26, 1999, at longitude 105 degrees, 30 minutes. It was a trial that none of us would forget. It may sound harsh, but the ritual was more fun than not. At the end we were a tighter crew, having gone through that time-honored ceremony together. Those Wogs have never been able to stomach another garbanzo bean, have guarded their Shellback certificates so they don't ever have to go through the hazing again, and still treasure the memories of that long eighteen-hour span.

After making it through the trials and tribulations, each Wog was eager to shed his skin and grow a shell on his back. Especially since that "skin" was an old T-shirt covered in stinking garbage, hot sauce, and other nameless delights. The fantail looked like a convention of male strippers, everyone flinging their clothes overboard and then getting a blast from the fire hose. It was a happy, tired, and bare bunch that reentered the ship—one united as trusty Shellbacks.

26.

JENNA IN PERIL DOWN UNDER

The bended knee is not a tradition of our Corps.

— General Alexander Vandegrift

ustralia is the promised land for sailors. The incredible sights, beautiful women who love American accents, and assertive beer were every sailor's dream. We were in the middle of the best cruise of my twenty-five-year career, and Australia was the cherry on top. But that cherry had a ticking bomb attached.

Jenna's life would be in jeopardy as soon as we docked, and she would be in harm's way for the duration of our stay.

We embarked two SH-60B Seahawk helicopters for this deployment. The helo detachment (HSL Det) was an essential part of the *Vandy* warfighting team. It was critical to meld the Det with the rest of the crew because the helos extended our lethality, and so we needed to operate together as a team. We also needed to be collegial; we would be living together on the ship for the next six months. A lieutenant commander was the Officer-in-Charge of four other pilots, three sensor operators, and ten maintenance technicians. The first challenge was finding space for these additional people and their stuff. Although the ship was built to support a Det, a frigate is like your garage; no unused space remained vacant for long.

Berthing was a touchy challenge. We had to move *Vandy* officers and enlisted sailors from their *permanent* racks to less desirable digs to make room for more-senior aviators. Having to move out of one's home, however compact it was, for six months did not sit well. This often led to a testy relationship between ship's company and the Det. It was natural to favor the crew, who was permanently assigned and would remain when the Det detached. But we had to forge a plan that made each side equally unhappy.

The Det moved aboard one dreary weekend, despondent about squeezing into a ship and dejected to be leaving home for half a year. One pilot found that his assigned rack was labeled "Jenna." Normally J. R.'s rack, it had been reassigned to this more senior pilot for the deployment. Confused by the female name, he inquired about who had previously slept in this bed. He was informed that he shared it with a dog. Thinking that he was the subject of a prank, he removed the label. Tempers flared, a spark lighting the tinder of resentment.

After a few minutes of heated argument, the pilot and his mates were escorted to the smoke deck. His eyes widened when he saw the red dog sitting amid the crew, looking expectantly from face to face. He approached slowly and knelt, offering his hand, clearly understanding canine etiquette. Jenna looked him up and down, sizing up the new guy. Then she shook her tail once and let herself be briefly petted. The pilot stood up and, grinning, shook hands with the bemused spectators. The tension was broken—and it would not return. Jenna had linked two separate entities into one team. She and her pilot got along famously for the next six months, as did the crew and the Det.

Tempers might have cooled, but the weather was hot without a cloud in sight. Having just crossed the equator, we had some blazing days left on our two-thousand-mile transit to Australia. I heard an odd rumor, so I made my way to the flight deck to check it out. The buzz turned out to be true: there was indeed a plastic kiddie pool on the flight deck. The helicopter dudes sat around a pool in foldable beach chairs, wearing flip-flops when they weren't flying or doing maintenance on the birds. I had to smile at the absurd scene of a bunch of twenty- to thirty-year-olds sitting in small aluminum chairs soaking their feet in a plastic pool emblazoned with clowns and balloons. They were on a Hawaiian beach, rather than in the middle of the ocean, in their minds.

I liked it and saw no reason to suppress their tiny independent commonwealth. Jenna visited this banana republic when in the area, but despite the humid heat resisted all attempts to get her into the pool. She was a real sailor, and sailors only get their feet wet if the ship sinks. She would find an open space between plastic-webbed lawn chairs and take a few laps—with her tongue. She didn't mind that feet dangled in the pool; this was pure spring water compared to the repugnant items she had wolfed down while crossing the line.

We had entered the Southern Hemisphere when we crossed the equator, which meant that we were upside down on the planet. Suddenly toilet water circled in the opposite direction, it got colder the further south we traveled, and there were strange and dangerous creatures everywhere. We landed in Darwin, at the northern tip of Australia. This was the Outback, home to kangaroos and backpackers but not to rain. Darwin was a small town with one main road, the perfect size for a frigate. This was not polished, urban Sydney, but more like an arid and scalding version of Anchorage. The locals were self-sufficient, outdoorsy, independent, proud—and they liked to have a beer or twelve. In other words, our kind of people.

Outside of the city we found red clay and struggling trees, everything covered by a blanket of fine red dust that would accumulate until next year's rain. Darwin was a frontier town containing locals proud of their autonomy amid a moon-like setting, a scattering of

European backpackers seeking a singular experience, and 225 sailors looking for a good time.

Local officials came aboard to welcome us and to provide port regulations. Among the standard discussions of town laws, off-limits establishments, and local sights, there was a shocker. They were quite happy to see lots of sailors who had three weeks of cash burning holes in their wallets but not thrilled to see a dog. Australia, like Hawaii, had quarantine laws to prevent rabies. But unlike Hawaii, they weren't about to overlook a dog no matter how cute she was. We had to purchase a high-priced bond to guarantee that Jenna would not leave the ship. But that was not the worst of it.

Officials warned us in no uncertain terms that they would *shoot Jenna* if she stepped foot off the ship!

Australia had great white sharks, huge saltwater crocs, and more venomous snakes than anywhere else in the world. If those did not get us, the box jellyfish or Tasmanian devil might. I wondered how they could be afraid of one small dog who had been quarantined at sea for weeks. I was eloquent, charming, and persuasive as I pled our case.

We put up the $10,000 bond.

This situation presented a real and present danger. As you know, Jenna was an escape artist who loved to wander. It was in her blood. That strict quarantine law, and the dire consequences of breaking it, put a damper on our plans. I looked around, wondering how to take care of this sticky problem. Lots of bewildered looks, this was a new dilemma for all of us. My eyes stopped at the Combat Systems Officer (CSO), who was doodling on his notepad. He had been struggling in his job and had yet to respond to counseling. And he clearly didn't grasp the magnitude of this situation.

He was *in the doghouse*. Hmmm...

CSO got the honor of putting up the bond and setting his own dog watch, which would last longer than the standard two hours. Days longer. I don't know how he guaranteed the money, but I do know that he stayed on board to protect his investment. Which gave him time to work on the problems in his department. Win-win, or lose-lose, depending on whose perspective it was. Whatever he did, and however he did it, worked. Escape artist Jenna did not leave the ship.

We were representatives of the United States when visiting foreign ports. Even a minor incident could blow up if the circumstances were right—or wrong. It would take just one newsman or local that didn't like the US presence, just one article in the paper or scathing letter to the embassy, or just one snippet that reached Admiral Blacker. I hoped that he had forgotten about us, or was too occupied to turn his all-seeing eyes toward us. All it would take would be one small reminder, followed by some staccato orders, and his aide would fly, fly to his pretty phone to make the call that would remove Jenna and our red ball caps. And end my career.

I imagined the Admiral sitting at a giant oak desk scanning Top Secret papers filed in color-coded folders.

His eyes glittered as he read an email from public affairs detailing our dog-related incident. A twisted smile crept onto his stern lips as he looked forward to thwacking the pesky fly that kept buzzing around in his brain. The Chief of Naval Operations might have let Jenna stay on the ship, but he would never know why Kusumoto's career hit a brick wall. It would feel so good closing the file on unfinished business and sending a stark signal that no one should step out of line.

I shook my head to clear these disquieting images. Don't overthink this. It could happen, but I could not make decisions based on how they might impact my own career.

We hosted a reception for local dignitaries and business leaders when we visited a new port, usually on the first night. Why? This was our small contribution to international relations and also set the crew up for a better port visit. It was extra work for Cody and the supply department, but they never complained.

The reception was held in the helicopter hanger, which was what I imagined the ballroom at the Ritz was like but with a few trifling differences. Instead of a gold and mauve color scheme, we had *fifty shades of gray*. We, too, had tall ceilings, and our bulkheads were ornamented with bulky aviation parts and red firefighting equipment. Certainly much more interesting than anything the Ritz could display. Our lighting was delightfully dim in places and harshly bright under the large industrial bulbs. The dark-gray sandpaper deck showcased the guests' shoes while roughening the bottoms and was much safer than slick Corinthian marble.

My sailors did their best to elegantly present drinks and hors d'oeuvres. Considering their lack of experience, eagerness to finish so they could hit the town, and their own increasing alcohol level, the service was credible. Our food was the finest available in the government supply system. I was thankful that the beef was not the fifty-first shade of gray. None of the guests cared after a few drinks. Laughter rose from every corner as guests and sailors got to know one another.

Not everyone was equal in the eyes of sailors. The crew sought to bond with the interesting people at the reception. Those included, in order of priority: bar owners, pretty women, bartenders, not-so-pretty women, heavy drinkers, and navy guys (a subset of the heavy drinkers). One of the Aussie sailors kept dropping his dentures into our beer cups, and we were then forced by avowed custom and peer pressure to drink the beer down, clutch his dentures with our teeth, and return them to him. Quarters or beer pong had nothing on that game, which added a nasty spin-the-bottle-trade-spit twist. I am not sure why that drinking game has not caught on in the US.

We reviled our Aussie naval brethren because they were allowed to drink alcohol on their ships. Little wonder that they had perfected drinking games during their months at sea, while we were watching *Groundhog Day* for the thirteenth time. In truth, it was clear to me that our ban on alcohol was a judicious rule. Keeping those spirits out of reach while we were bored and tired was appropriate and necessary.

We had gathered the gouge (information) we needed after two hours of bland American beer and self-assembled *pupus*. The local bar and restaurant owners handed out drink coupons and would fly *Welcome US Navy* banners outside of their establishments. Golf courses, hotels, and other places of entertainment were at our command. And I had met the governor, sheriff, police chief, and other local officials. If—when—someone got in trouble, I knew who to call.

Jenna also made the rounds, charming and ingratiating, floating about like a mini-Killer Tomato. She would look up with a sweet face until someone dispensed an hors d'oeuvre. *Gulp*, on to the next guest. She was a political animal, meeting and greeting, getting what she wanted, then moving on—until she got to Olivia, a statuesque owner of an Irish bar.

"Get out of town!" Olivia squealed. "They've got a *dog*!"

Jenna backed up a step, sensing drama. She eyed the woman cautiously.

"For real? It's just like in those American pictures."

"She's our mascot; her name is Jenna," quipped the XO, conveniently at her side.

Olivia crouched down toward Jenna, her already tight dress stretched across her bum. Jenna was frozen, somehow affixed to the deck by this brassy intrusion.

Olivia patted Jenna on the top of the head once...twice... and then a third time. The XO and nearby crew winced once...twice...thrice. They knew that Jenna did not like to be touched, and she loathed being patted on the head. Jenna also winced, momentarily stunned, then turned and trotted away. She shot a dark glance over her shoulder at the cheeky visitor.

"Well, she sure is sweet," Olivia said, straightening up and smoothing her dress. "You boys should bring her with you to my bar."

The XO dragged his eyes away from her now smooth dress and nodded.

Australia lived up to our fantasies. This land down under, populated with native people and European exports, contained incredible natural beauty, diversity, and national pride. And an abundance of strong beer and beautiful women. It was familiar enough to make us comfortable, yet different enough to be interesting. We left with great memories, wistfully looking over our shoulders. Jenna, however, left without getting to meet a kangaroo. But she met lots of Aussies who came aboard on tours and was an unexpected treat for those visitors. By the end of our stay, there would have been a local outcry had she been shot for escaping the ship.

The CSO may have been the happiest of all; he left without having to pay a $10,000 quarantine fine.

27.

LIBERTY HOUNDS

Partying 'Cause It's 1999.

— Apologies to Prince

We were men-at-arms, sailors who in earlier times would have been feared for sacking and plundering the ports we entered. But now *we* came to be plundered, to squander our paychecks on trinkets and ale. Mainly ale. We spent hundreds of dollars while on liberty, often a full paycheck, and departed with a T-shirt now two sizes too small.

And with memories.

Fond memories of good times, late into the night, with friends old and new.

Confused memories of waking up in new and unexpected places.

We were liberty hounds, panting to go ashore. We waited many days and nights at sea to finally pierce the tight channel and blissfully burst into a new port. Each day our eagerness grew as we discussed planned excursions. Newbies gathered around grizzled thirty-year-old veterans who tried to trump one another's tales of past exploits. It was a live travel program that imparted the gouge on where to go and what to do once you got there. Although McDonald's and Starbucks had infested every city, each port remained unique, each an exotic temptress that excited and captivated.

When we stopped in Guam for fuel on our transit from San Diego to Japan, the Admiral there gave me a hot tip that the neighboring island of Saipan made for a great port visit. I remembered his advice and was eventually able to finagle a visit to Saipan. This island is only twelve miles long by five miles across, but those sixty square miles contain incredible cliffs, limestone forests, sandy beaches, and one incredible grotto. A poor man's Hawaii, in 1999 it had only been discovered by a few Japanese tourists and remained untarnished. As a commonwealth of the United States, the locals spoke English and used American dollars, so no translation of language or currency was required. The Admiral had not lied.

Land Ho! When the lookout spotted land, the rails quickly became crowded. Sailors gazed across the sea, making wishes and plans. At first the city was just a blur in the distance, but it gradually took shape. Jenna maneuvered between dungaree-clad legs, sticking her head between the lifelines to get a look and an unadulterated sniff. She took long, deep breaths, her head still and eyes steady as she took in the island through her nose. After a few minutes, she tipped her tail, as close to a wag as she could manage, and allowed crouched shipmates a few minutes of petting.

The mottled green peaks of the island lanced the vivid blue sky, the sparkling water so clear we could see multitudes of fish as we entered port. We spotted a welcoming committee led by the mayor and Miss Saipan as we approached the pier. Guess which one the crew was most interested in. The beautiful girl in the sash was a short-lived pleasure, while the mayor turned out to be a fantastic host. He invited the officers and chiefs to his home for dinner.

Thirty of us climbed the hill to his official residence overlooking the harbor and were surprised to find the mayor's wife and many daughters preparing heaping bowls of local food. We devoured the delectable home-cooked banquet, enjoying warm Chamorro hospitality. After digesting the feast, we browsed the various plaques and pictures on the walls. It was astonishing to find that this house had been occupied by Navy commanders who governed the island until 1978, part of the US Navy's one-hundred-year governance of the Marianas.

Saipan was much more than a vacation spot. There was serious history here. The World War II Battle of Saipan, fought as the Navy and Marine Corps rolled back Japanese forces one island at a time, was one of the bloodiest victories in our history. US forces lost thirty-six hundred men during that three-week battle, which is comparable to US combat deaths during the nine year Iraq War. The Japanese fought to the last man; fewer than one thousand of their thirty thousand soldiers survived.

Suicide Cliff is one of the most dramatic locations in the world, a sheer bluff dropping hundreds of feet. Hundreds, possibly thousands of Japanese soldiers and civilians jumped to their deaths here rather than be captured. In total, some twenty thousand Japanese civilians perished on Saipan. As I stood near the small commemorative placard at Suicide Cliff, looking at the sea and valley far below and feeling my stomach clench from the height, it was difficult to imagine the circumstances that compelled so many to leap to their death. It was at once beautiful and tragic, a rare spot on Earth.

The Grotto on the island stands alone among my mental postcards. A weathered piece of wood with "Grotto" roughly carved into it marked a narrow red-dirt path. After hiking a short distance, I exited scrub brush to look down upon a breathtaking scene. A large circular hole in the top of white limestone cliffs revealed a deep blue pool below. Light filtered up from three underwater tunnels connecting the grotto to the ocean, backlighting the large cavern from below. A surge from unseen waves pushed water upward through the tunnels against the rocks, then receded in rhythm with the ocean swell. I climbed down wet and slippery cement steps that were at a steep angle, demanding that I pry my eyes from the cobalt circle below and concentrate on keeping my footing. I ditched my T-shirt and shoes on a boulder.

At the bottom I jumped into the pool from a large boulder ten feet above the surface, timing my leap with the outgoing swell to ensure I was not smashed back against the rocks. I treaded water while slowly rotating 360 degrees, taking in this unparalleled spot. Moping bystanders who lacked time or swim gear gazed forlornly at the beatific scene. The water was warm and crystal clear. The bottom seemed close enough to reach out and touch, but it was twenty feet down. Swimmers enjoyed the unique setting, floating serenely with the interior tide while gazing up at stalactites hanging from the limestone cliffs. Snorkelers gazed at butterfly fish, barracuda, or even reef sharks swimming close.

Sharks?

My brain knew they were harmless, but when in the water with them I feared I might encounter that one mentally disturbed shark. Scuba divers swam down through the tunnels to explore reefs and caves sixty feet down. We warned the crew that people died periodically at The Grotto. The strong current trapped divers in the caves; it was not a place to cool off after a six-pack. Most of the crew visited this landmark. Even now, mention of The Grotto brings instant smiles and sunbaked stories.

In the evening, the XO and I took Jenna for a long walk to explore the compact town and see what our sailors were up to. A humid breeze rustled palm fronds overhead, and a tanned hand waved from a rusty red

VW Bug as it sputtered by. A mix of local islanders and tourists ambled along the one-lane main street, the tropical air sedating them into a contented stupor. The merchants had an Aloha spirit of their own, selling knickknacks without hassle. I watched as American greenbacks traded hands. Seafood from the surrounding ocean was the main course in most restaurants, but an influx of Japanese tourists to this "half-off Hawaii" had given rise to sushi bars and teppanyaki restaurants. As always, Jenna attracted attention. People stopped us to pet her, which she tolerated with lowered head and tail at half-mast. She was more responsive to the store owners who offered her dog biscuits, which she considered minimum wage for putting up with all the unwanted attention.

As we turned the corner onto a side street, I spied a few crew members across the street. They were walking briskly and did not notice us. Just as I was about to hail them, they stopped at a doorway, exchanged a few words with a large man sitting on a three-legged stool, and slipped inside. The place was the size of a main street furniture store, but there was no signage and the display windows were painted flat black.

Curious...

We crossed the street, and I tied Jenna to one of the plumeria trees that lined the street. She laid down, happy to remain in the open air. The large Samoan in the doorway waved us inside with a knowing grin. We smiled back and sauntered in. The first thing we saw

was a large elevated platform, barren except for a tat-
tered pink couch and one lone chair. High-wattage
overhead lights scorched the "stage" and illuminated
sailors seated at tables below.

Strip club!

A performer sauntered out. She motioned to the
crowd, and the announcer asked for a volunteer to join
her on stage. Quicker than a speeding bullet a young
petty officer made his way onto the stage, drunkenly
swaying to the music. This was a corrupted version of
hula dancers bringing tourists on stage to attempt awkward hula moves. The sailor hobbled up to the "host" like
a Chippendale—the horse, not one of the famous male
strippers. He was uninhibited, oblivious to our presence
and enjoying his moment in the spotlight. His clothes
came off much faster than the female's, aaaaaaannnnd
it was time to leave.

The bouncer was sitting on the curb next to Jenna,
both watching the sparse pedestrian traffic. He smiled
at us and gently petted Jenna with his massive brown
hand, then returned to his post. We untied Jenna and
headed back to the ship, trying to get the floppy pink
images out of our heads. I looked at Steve, and he tilted
his head sideways and popped his top ear with his palm
as if trying to force the images out of the other ear. It
didn't work; the images were burned in. I snickered, he
snorted as he attempted to retain control, and soon *we*
were sitting on the curb trying to catch our breath from
a bout of hysterical laughing. Jenna sat sphinxlike, dark

eyes fixed on us. I gave her a hug, feeling the slight resistance of her leaning away.

"Jenna, you're lucky you didn't see what we saw!"

"Yeah," Steve said, "or else you'd have to poke your own eyes out."

I looked at Steve, and we started chuckling again.

At breakfast the next day someone mentioned that *60 Minutes* had been filming in town last night, and they had interviewed Petty Officer Kirk Hawk. Visions of drunk-naked-enthusiastic-drunk-hairy-flabby sailors danced in my head. I looked over at the XO, who raised his eyebrows then sank his chin onto his chest in mock exasperation. Kirk would one day become a Master Chief, one of the senior leaders in the ranks. But at that moment he was young and brash, having just joined the ship. I wasn't sure what he might have said to the famous investigative reporting team, especially if it was after a few (hundred) beers. Unwanted images of the strip club entered my head, sending a shiver up my spine. I never obtained a clear picture of what was said or to whom, but I also never saw a clear picture of any of my sailors on *60 Minutes*. Not that there was anything inappropriate going on...

As usual, the crew ended up congregating in a few select bars. Dave's Bar, a midsize joint with darts and TVs, became a favorite. Yes, darts and TVs and beer were all it took to make sailors happy. Dave treated us like neighborhood friends, and the crew returned his hospitality by spending many hours in his bar. It didn't hurt that his attractive waitresses served reasonably priced drinks. Closing time, as decreed by law, arrived way too soon. Was it 2:00 a.m. already?

Dave complied with the law.

Sort of.

He informed me that he could no longer sell alcohol. He put a hand on my shoulder as I started to rise, walked to the door, and locked it. As we stared at him, at least the few who were paying attention, he turned and announced that since he couldn't legally sell any more beer it was now *on the house*.

What?!

This was something I had not experienced in all my decades in bars. A loud cheer went up! Beer was poured, and I was proud to see the crew pony up wads of cash for a "tip." I'm certain Dave made out in the informal exchange, but I am equally certain that was not his intent.

We returned to Saipan a few months later when a port visit to Guadalcanal was cancelled. This was a stroke of good fortune for Petty Officer Jim Hedge. At six foot four he looked like a giant redwood in his small office, where he ensured we had the right supplies to keep the ship running. He was fair and sandy-haired, with a ready smile and gentle demeanor. As befit his leadership style of actions not words, he had accompanied Chris Mirabella and Shane Celesky on liberty during our previous visit. The two young seamen had gotten

NEAL J. KUSUMOTO, CAPTAIN, US NAVY (RET)

into trouble ashore the night before, so Jim decided to provide adult supervision and act as a role model.

Good deeds do pay off! During their run ashore, the boys stopped at Club GIG, a large disco that accommodated 350 people. Jim met Lyn, a beautiful, petite, dark-haired local girl working there. Fireworks exploded... fireworks that still light their skies, though now in Texas. When we returned to Saipan, Jim was ecstatic. He and Lyn spent every minute together and then continued their long-distance relationship until they were married three years later. They are still married twenty-three years later and have a son.

Unlikely that love could be found in a bar during a brief stop? Perhaps, but not more so than any other scene. I met my wife, Linda, in a bar during a port visit to San Francisco, and we too have lived happily ever after. So when you spot sailors walking down the streets of your city, see them not just as young adults looking for a good time—though that would not be inaccurate—but also as young warriors, ambassadors, and potential in-laws.

Every city was different, every city was the same. Each had its own look and vibe, but people everywhere want to love, to live, and to be happy. We left each port with a mixture of sadness and relief. We missed the exotic, slightly dangerous clandestine adventure...a kind of one-night stand without regrets. But we were also bushed from long nights, different cultures, and unfamiliar foods. It was like returning home from spending

Christmas week with distant family; we had a great time but were thankful to get some shuteye in our own racks. I still treasure the memories of each unique port of call. The sounds and sights remain a vivid menagerie in my mind's eye, and the tastes and the smells are still sweet and pungent.

As the ship departed, all eyes gazed back at Saipan in quiet reverie—an incredibly beautiful island with a history of so much death. Jenna sat a few feet from me, eyes barely open and nose quivering. A humid breeze ruffled her red coat. As we hit open water, I could not know that our most dangerous challenge lay ahead. One that would put the ship, even our lives, at risk.

28.

CHANNEL FEVER

It follows then as certain as that
night succeeds the day,
that without a decisive naval force
we can do nothing definitive,
and with it, everything honorable and glorious.

— President George Washington

E very deployment is a chapter in the life of a ship. It is also a chapter in the lives of sailors and their families. We were having fun while in port, but that accounted for less than 5 percent of the deployment. We were missing our families 100 percent of the time. As our deployment dragged on for four... five...six months, geographic separation created an emotional chasm that couples would have to negotiate. But first we had to get home, which was going to be the most dangerous part of our long voyage.

We had fun and games during our deployment, but the day-to-day reality was hard work, long hours, and little rest or relaxation. Returning from deployment was like Christmas morning as a child. Anticipation built up for months, and we were ready to burst by the time we reached home. The prolonged separation was intensified by being limited to a handful of times when we could communicate during the last half year. Remember that this was in the dark ages before cell phones. Sailors might as well have been in a coma for six months. Instead of seeing themselves as part of the family movie, they had to create internal snapshots of all the things that they had missed: babies growing up...graduations, ball games, and plays...new songs, TV shows, movies, and styles...engagements, weddings, separations, and divorces (hopefully not theirs)...births, birthdays, funerals...new jobs, lost ones, promotions, and demotions...church, vacations, trips, and mini-adventures...storms, sunshine, snow, wind, rain...problems with the house, car, kids, neighbors, or parents.

Maybe even a new dog.

We couldn't wait to hear, in person, about our families' adventures and trials. We longed to see the twinkle or tears in their eyes as they recounted all the important events we had missed and to see family photos...even though they did not include us.

Smiles widened when our mission was complete, and we turned the ship toward home port. It would be weeks until we saw loved ones on the pier, but at least we were headed in the right direction. This, paradoxically, was the most dangerous part of the deployment. Although

Vandy was no longer refueling from a giant aircraft carrier or avoiding Chinese ships at flank speed, the threat of an accident multiplied as the crew relaxed and minds drifted from duty to home. Collisions, groundings, incidents ashore—all occur more frequently during the homestretch.

As the captain, it was my job to keep us running *through* the finish line rather than mentally relaxing as we approached the tape. I understood the risk and had to safeguard against it without quenching the joy and excitement of going home. My first step was to cut out duties that weren't absolutely necessary in order to focus on critical functions like watch standing, safety, and equipment maintenance. If some cleaning or administrative duties weren't perfect, so be it.

Anticipation grew day by day, and in the final days it felt like the week before Christmas—except without the shopping or decorations or special food. We did have a couple of semi-jolly pudgy men doing mandatory exercise so they could pass the next physical fitness test. Sky-high expectations pushed worries aside but, like Christmas, the actual event sometimes did not live up to the storybook video in our heads.

Jenna was keenly attuned to the crew. Her tail was held high as she walked the decks, and she even paused—occasionally—to be petted. I watched as sailors bent and talked softly to her. Were they sharing their joy of going home? Perhaps secret fears of what they might find? Whatever the confidences were, each sailor smiled as if absolved. And Jenna never betrayed their trust.

We celebrated Channel Fever Night on the evening before pulling into home port. We were like kids on Christmas Eve who were too excited to sleep, impatiently waiting to unwrap our presents. Which in this case were our wives or girlfriends. Sailors congregated to sit around and talk, watch a movie, or play cards. The only ones working were those standing watch to ensure we got home in one piece. Jenna roamed the mess decks, looking for handouts. Each sailor gently ran his hand along her back as she passed his blue plastic chair. She eventually curled up on her small rug in the corner, head on tail and eyes watching the uncharacteristic commotion.

The night passed s-l-o-w-l-y, as endless as a winter night at the North Pole.

At last, morning beckoned as the stars lost brilliance against the gray dawn. The ocean materialized, white lines drawn upon its opaque canvas by small waves. Finally, the sun appeared and drew the curtain back. I was sitting in my chair on the starboard bridge wing contemplating our imminent entry into Japanese waters. It was a beautiful day, not a cloud in the sky, and a slight breeze that barely ruffled the water. Jenna was sitting below me enjoying the early sun, back legs splayed, ears perked, eyes closed but twitching nose betraying her attentiveness. I tried to imagine the amazing array of sea smells that she was enjoying, a rainbow of sensations invisible to me. Did she smell a pod of oceanic dolphins that had hunted in this area, or perhaps giant tuna that had leaped after prey in the early hours?

Today we were transiting one of the busiest and riskiest waterways in the world. The USS *Fitzgerald* would have a disastrous collision here in 2017, killing seven sailors. *Vandy* had company, lots of it. This waterway into Tokyo also led to Yokohama, Chiba, Kawasaki, and Yokosuka, ports that were themselves among the busiest in Asia. Huge tankers, boxy roll-on roll-off car carriers, container ships, Navy craft of both nations, coastal freighters, and fishermen were all here in large numbers. Of all the difficult places I have navigated—Hong Kong, Shanghai, Singapore, Inchon, La Rochelle, Porto—this was the most stressful despite having done it dozens of times. The crew was focused on home, could almost touch it, which further elevated the risk factor in this final fifty-mile stretch.

Fortunately, conditions were good. Negligible wind and seas, with excellent visibility. A perfect day except for the rush-hour traffic. It was the maritime equivalent of bumper-to-bumper, except instead of being slow and tedious, it raised me to my toe tops as I scanned ahead, beside, and behind us. Many of these ships, much larger than *Vandy*, were going twenty knots. Time was money to them, and speed improved their maneuverability. It would take them at least ten minutes, or three miles, to bring their hurtling bulk to a stop. Think of a fully loaded timber truck rumbling down a steep, narrow mountain road with the last load of the day. You better not plan on him stopping or swerving to avoid you.

Make no mistake, although there was no pavement or dividing line drawn, we were on a highway delineated by shallow water on both sides. As the volcanic Mount Daisen rose off our starboard side, we merged with another major route from the south. This was the equivalent of two major interstates merging just before entering a city, rather than splitting off some of the traffic onto a beltway.

We entered this funnel into Tokyo Bay twenty miles from our home port of Yokosuka, surrounded on all sides by ships. Like driving on a highway, it was safer to keep up with traffic, and so we were also making twenty knots. This was much faster than our normal transit speed of twelve knots.

Increasing speed increased risk. If we lost an engine, we might have trouble maintaining twenty knots. Imagine driving your car on a highway where it would take ten minutes for any vehicle around you to stop. If we had a casualty and lost steering or speed, we'd be in trouble. We would have little time to react and fewer options because of the traffic density and speed. To make matters worse, our high speed had also taken away my option to anchor in an emergency.

There was no room for error.

No shoulder to pull onto and slow down. No way to slow with the enormous tankers tailgating us.

My heart pumped hard against my chest.

I edged the ship to the far-left edge of our inbound lane, which was on the right side of the channel similar to US car lanes. This meant I had to avoid the huge buoys marking the center of the channel, but it allowed me to prepare for our left turn into Yokosuka. Now came the riskiest part—we had to turn left and dash across a half mile of oncoming traffic, also crowded and at high speed, with smaller ships shielded from view by larger ones. Imagine driving down your nearest highway, doing sixty-five miles per hour with cars beside and behind you, and having to time your arrival at an exact spot to make a left turn across heavy oncoming traffic. And no one has brakes.

That's what we had to do.

I was sweating internally. I did my best to maintain a cool demeanor, to stay calm and carry on. I glanced down to find Jenna lying on the cool deck, watching with sleepy interest. I knelt and stroked her shoulders and back, then scratched behind her ears. I would like to say that she closed her eyes contentedly, but by now you know that Jenna was not an ordinary "people dog." I did close *my* eyes and took a series of deep breaths. My heart slowed and my jaw relaxed...a little.

Be like Jenna, cool and collected.

It was important to let everyone do their job without ratcheting up the stress level. I got into my chair and put my feet on the rail, fighting the urge to be everywhere at once.

My serenity was short-lived, though the bridge team was less edgy. Good thing. This was a dicey evolution that, if it went wrong, could lead to casualties or even deaths. Normally we could slow and wait for an opportunity to cross the channel, but not today. If we slowed, we would be run over by the giant ships riding our tail. I scanned ahead, watching the outbound traffic as it came into view around a point of land a few miles ahead. I was looking for a gap, praying for one that was big enough that we could sprint through like a running back.

At the last minute I spied it. There was a slight gap, more like a crease, but we had to make our move.

Flank speed! Left full rudder!

The gas turbines wound up as we rapidly reached twenty-eight knots, heeling over into a sharp turn. We aimed at a tanker on the far side of the outgoing traffic. Yes, we aimed directly at another ship...I said it was a *crease*. Although we pointed our bow at him, his relative motion would ensure we passed astern of him. Smiles broke out until we spotted a small coastal freighter that had been hidden on the other side of our target ship. He was going slower, and we had a constant bearing and decreasing range to him.

Which meant that we were on a collision course.

I had seconds to decide. There was no time to slow due to the other ships coming down on us. I was earning my three-dollar command responsibility pay today.

We turned right and went the WRONG way up the channel, heading directly into heavy traffic. I watched our relative motion, and after a hair-raising minute, we made a sharp left to pass close astern of the nearest ship and just ahead of the oncoming tanker right behind it. I closed my eyes and realized that I had been holding my breath.

Jenna barked loudly twice. We all turned in surprise, and then laughed too loudly in relief. She was staring at the closest ship, legs stiff, hackles raised. Jenna turned from looking at the freighter and scanned our faces, then returned to her perch at the base of my chair.

We now had a calm mile before we entered Yokosuka Bay, which was much less congested. We blasted "We Like to Party" by the Vengaboys, our deployment song, over the ship's loudspeakers. It brought flashbacks of an incredible cruise conducting the Navy's business and having a great time doing it. We flew our huge battle ensign for the first time since Shanghai. The crew was manning the rails in their white uniforms, looking forward to hugs, kisses, homecoming parties, and surprises with their family and friends.

Jenna was carried down the ladders and wandered among the crew on the forecastle, tail a blondish-red pennant in the breeze. We entered the narrow channel into Yokosuka, Mount Fuji majestic on the Kantō Plain ahead, then made the final turn into our pier. We navigated toward a pier that held a large, faded-blue tent festooned with blue and gold balloons. Families were straining to find the faces of loved ones as we got closer, and *Vandy* sailors sporting enormous grins were waving their hands in high arcs. If only we could have captured that moment, bottled the excitement and pent-up emotions of six months of accumulated stress and uncertainty being shattered by happiness and anticipation. The happiness that soared far above the freed balloons. The anticipation and hunger that could not be sated by the food served on the pier. The rippling anxiety to see what had changed since we left.

So we were finally home.

All those dreams of family and friends, of all the things we missed while we were gone—all of it was finally within our grasp. But reality seldom lives up to dreams, and even Christmas morning quickly becomes more about cleaning up the paper than enjoying the gifts. At first there were tears, hugs, kisses. It was almost impossible to physically or verbally express the love and relief each person felt. After hugging and kissing their dads, the kids ran to see Jenna, who was tethered to one of the benches. Kids, crowds, tether—she was not in her happy place. But she stood there and bore all the attention, the kids oblivious to her downcast tail. She was the perfect halftime entertainment that got them past the interlude between the blissful welcome and when things returned to normal, that nether region between pure happiness and real life.

Soon enough, reality hit. The party was over too quickly and real life barged in. Things had changed and life had somehow gone on without us. The invisible lines of demarcation between spouses had shifted, the wife taking on the alpha role in our absence. Though unexpected and unwelcome, it made sense. She had to take sole leadership and management of the family; she had done her job and ours while we were gone. After a six-month deployment, physically separated with infrequent communications and support, couples with strong bonds stretched and gained flexibility while weaker ones frayed or broke. She was glad to see her husband and tried to understand the hardships he had been through—but she had been through her *own deployment*, running a sovereign family-nation. All those things we normally took care of, she had done, by herself. And now we had returned, ready to jump back into the role we had vacated. But that didn't happen seamlessly.

We had been absent, why should we get to start making the decisions now?

Most Navy wives were already independent, but absence made them self-sufficient. In addition, the children had grown and now looked to their mothers for guidance. Best not to ask too many questions, nothing that could be construed as criticism. Something as bland as, "Why is the dishwasher making that noise?" sounded a lot like, "Why haven't you kept things up around here?" Boundary lines were reestablished, though not exactly as they had been. Love and intimacy were the balm that took the sting out and that allowed wounds to heal.

Most of the crew brought their families to visit the ship to see where Daddy had lived while he was away for so long. They got to see where he worked and experience the metal confines where he lived. There was so little in common between the gray ship and their warm house, such a difference in their father's work routine and their daily schedule at home. Fortunately, there was a red tie that bound these two lifestyles.

Jenna.

She was a red coat of domesticity splashed across a hard gray landscape. The cute furry dog, no matter how aloof, was the only soft thing on the ship. She was always a hit with the children, providing a common point between sailor and family. A sailor could say things through Jenna that were hard for him to express. With one arm around his fascinated child and the other reaching out toward Jenna, it was easier to say, "Jenna and I missed you so much." Or, "Jenna is worried about you and wants to hear what's wrong." Families returned often to see Jenna, usually when Dad had to stay on board during his duty day. The ship became a positive experience for the family rather than just the vehicle that took Daddy away.

29.

ONE DOG'S LEGACY

Every dog must have its day.

— Jonathan Swift

enna walked with a purpose, head high, foxy triangular ears erect, Spitz-tail curled upon her back. She was a proud Shiba Inu—an ancient breed specialized to guard palaces—and she didn't harbor fools. No cuddly dog, this one. Pet her and she endured it, but reclined ears signaled her irritation. Hug her or pick her up and she'd squirm to be released. Jenna was all business; she had no time to chase balls or play tug-of-war.

This proud pound dog served for five years on USS *Vandegrift*, which equated to thirty-five "dog years" of consecutive sea duty. A sailor has a two- to six-year tour on a ship and then spends four to six years ashore for some downtime. Thirty-five years must be a record, but there is no historical documentation on canine sea service.

Jenna made it clear when it was finally time for her to detach from the ship. I and most of the original crew had transferred, and although our replacements quickly became friendly shipmates, it was time for well-deserved shore duty. She bypassed the requisite paperwork, communicating her decision to retire in the only way she knew how.

She went AWOL whenever she got the chance.

Shiba Inus are notorious escape artists. Crafty and quick, Jenna was true to her breed. It only took a moment when the quarterdeck watch's attention was diverted and she'd be gone, blowing across the brow and loping down the pier to explore the base. She would eventually show up at the Pickenses' house. Slim had transferred from the ship but was still stationed in Yokosuka. He dutifully brought her back to the ship, and she returned to his house at her next opportunity. It was obvious that she no longer wanted to live on the ship. The crew wanted to keep her, but as fellow sailors they understood that she had more than met her commitment.

Jenna's transfer ashore was regretfully approved.

The crew spent more and more time with Jenna as her departure neared. She was an icon in the fleet and a fixture on the ship, having been on board longer than anyone else. Her life on board *Vandy* had been historic, and it seemed wrong that she should leave the ship without fanfare. When an officer detaches, the Wardroom assembles on the quarterdeck and forms a funnel. The outgoing person walks through parallel lines of officers, shaking hands and exchanging parting remarks. At the end of the line, he salutes the captain, who gives him permission to go ashore. The watch stander bongs the officer ashore as he crosses the gangplank, no longer part of ship's company.

When Jenna arrived at the quarterdeck for her final departure, on a leash to prevent an abbreviated ceremony, there was a column of well-wishers. It was the longest column in ship's history, by far. The funnel was not limited to officers as per tradition, but also included enlisted crew members who wanted to honor her and say good-bye.

It was a long, red funnel; each sailor standing at attention was wearing a red ball cap. The ball caps, like Jenna, had survived Admiral Blacker's "suggestion" to remove them so many years ago.

I too had survived, avoiding retribution for keeping Jenna on board.

As Jenna sauntered down the line, she seemed to know it was her day. For once she was in no hurry, head high and tail curled so the tip touched her back. She looked each sailor in the eye as they petted her and said their goodbyes. There must have been dust in the wind, because sailors don't cry. She reached the captain, who saluted and thanked her for her exemplary duty. He then gave her permission to go ashore *one last time*.

Two bongs were sounded, followed by "Seaman Jenna, departing" over the loudspeakers.

When she reached the pier, a spontaneous cheer went up as the crew waved their red ball caps in a final farewell.

Little did anyone know that, eight years later and 5,600 miles away, Jenna would be bonged back aboard the USS *Vandegrift*.

Jenna transferred to the Pickens family and then moved to Texas when Slim moved to a new duty station. Two years later, Slim received new orders to return to Japan. Jenna was eleven years old, and the 6,500-mile journey would have been too much for her. As luck would have it, my wife, Linda, and I had just moved to Corpus Christi and lived only a few miles from Slim. We jumped at the chance to take Jenna.

The day finally arrived when Jenna was to report aboard. The wind smashed raindrops into the windows, and thunderclaps followed sharp flashes every few minutes. I jumped up several times, thinking I heard a car pulling into our driveway. Finally, the doorbell rang. I opened the door to Slim holding a wet, squirming red dog.

"Ohhh, she looks just like a red fox!" exclaimed Linda.

Jenna still looked good. Her red coat was full, her tail curved and bushy, her eyes bright and intelligent. And she clearly had lots of energy, struggling against being held. A few gray hairs had sprouted under her chin, and when Slim put her down, she stretched her back legs. I grabbed a towel and dried Jenna. She stopped squirming as she smelled my arms, then looked at my face. I let her go. She rubbed the side of her head against my knees and let out a soft moan, and I was surprised to see her tail start a low wag.

She then did the inconceivable.

Jenna rolled over onto her back, exposing her belly. Her mouth was open, exposing her teeth as if in a huge grin. She pumped her front paws into the air, then went quiet as I lightly scratched her ribcage. Tongue lolling out to the side and eyes glazed, she was a picture of contentment...or lunacy.

I looked up at Slim, whose eyes were wide. He pursed his lips and shrugged.

I continued scratching, and Jenna lay in a comatose state for a few seconds more. Then her eyes focused, and she got to her feet. She stood ramrod straight, tail curved onto her back, a slight inquisitive tilt to her head as she looked into my eyes.

I returned her stare, then smiled and said, "It's OK, girl, have a look around!"

Jenna smirked and trotted off to explore her new house.

"I thought you said she wasn't very friendly," Linda said.

"Yeah, right!" said Slim. "I've never seen her act like this."

I shook my head, watching her nose around. Clearly, she remembered me. What else of her life at sea did she recall?

Did she ever dream of being back on the ship, like I did?

Jenna lived a quiet life with us for her last six years. Although she mellowed as her chin grayed, she remained sharp and "on watch." She patrolled her outside domain, which consisted of a large yard with a koi pond, a deck, and a dock. She learned to fish, which in her case meant snatching a wriggling speckled trout from my line as I brought it onto the dock. She sat by the koi pond for hours watching the big fish swim, trying to figure out how to grab one. They swam up to the side of the pond when I came around, thinking it was time to be fed. Jenna leaned out as far out as possible, stretching to get a whiff of them. She would not get her feet wet, so the koi were safe.

Jenna quickly figured out the signs that indicated we were preparing to take the boat for a spin. She would stay close to me, clearly intent on getting underway for a short cruise. Once we got the boat launched, Jenna would stand at attention in the bow, a red-haired figurehead with nose high to catch every scent. She'd lie down on a seat when her aging legs tired, front legs crossed in a relaxed pose yet still taking it all in. These short cruises were part-time mascot work for her, with a mini-crew.

Jenna maintained a love-hate relationship with her leash. She hated to be constrained, wanting to run free as she had on the base in Japan. But she also loved to sniff new places and perhaps exchange a quick, noncommittal greeting with another dog. So she was excited when the leash made an appearance but twisted her neck to avoid the collar. Although her mind was always willing, the walks grew shorter each year. She could still run and jump but was stiff and sore the next day.

Jenna eased into retirement, resting her bones in the shade until some wayward blue heron trespassed on her dock. She learned the art of siesta, dozing in a shady spot on the cool tile during the hot hours of summer. We bought her a waterbed that cushioned her joints and bones, and kept her cool. She loved it and would use no other bed for the rest of her life. After two years in Texas, we moved to San Diego, where Jenna lived out her final years.

30.

JENNA COME HOME!

Twenty years from now you will
be more disappointed
by the things that you didn't do
than by the ones you did do.
So throw off the bowlines. Sail
away from the safe harbor.
Catch the trade winds in your sails.
Explore. Dream. Discover.

— H. JACKSON BROWN JR.

The captain of the *Vandegrift* called me in 2010. The ship had returned to San Diego from Japan, and he had discovered that Jenna was not only still alive, but she also lived in San Diego. He said the legend of Jenna had been kept alive over the past seven years. More than just kept alive, Jenna remained relevant to daily life on board. One of the questions on the Enlisted Surface Warfare Qualification test was to name the former mascot. More surprising was that the ship's covert password for shipboard security was

"Seaman Jenna" and would remain so until the ship was decommissioned.

His crew wanted to meet Jenna.

Badly.

One sunny weekday morning Linda and I loaded Jenna into the car. As always, she moved to the back of the SUV to prop herself against the lift back. That old sea dog knew to brace for potential rough waters. Once we were on a steady course and speed, she moved to the window to check the canine wireless network flowing on the airstream. When we entered the naval base, she perked up, ears trained forward and head stretched out as far as possible. We heard a slight hum as the back window went all the way down, and I saw in the side-view mirror that she had extended her body halfway out of the window. Linda twisted around and pulled her back, then closed the window to the halfway position again. This was not the first time that Jenna had pressed the window button with her paw, a trick she must have learned from the crew.

Was it just the sea air, or was it the familiar smells of the ships that excited her?

What memories did they trigger?

Although fourteen years old, Jenna was still mobile and lucid. Her nose twitched and she whined. Whined? Linda and I exchanged surprised glances.

We pulled up to the congested pier, parking at a spot reserved for Seaman Jenna. As we walked down the pier to the ship, the sights and sounds and smells fired up my brain cells. Memories of twenty-five years in the Navy, of my years in command of this ship, of all the port calls and training exercises. This was the same pier that I had walked down twelve years ago when I reported to *Vandy* as her new captain, and I thought of all the water that had passed beneath her keel since then. A dozen years ago I had reported aboard with an endless horizon stretching ahead, and today I visited as a civilian with a desk job.

I thought of all my shipmates who had served on this fine ship, of all the adventures we had together. I found it hard to swallow due to an unexpected lump in my throat. Walking with Jenna and Linda by my side, one an old hand and the other new to Navy life aboard ship, was a surreal stroll past the routine hustle and bustle of sailors working on ships. Jenna walked with ears and tail high, not perturbed by the moving machinery, loud sounds, or oily odors of a working pier. *This was not her first Navy pier*, not by a long shot.

Who could have foreseen this moment, so many years ago, when we enlisted a small red dog from a shelter in Japan?

When we arrived at the brow, they bonged four bells and announced, "Captain, United States Navy retired, arriving." Then two bells and, "Seaman Jenna, returning." The captain stood waiting, smiling and saluting as I requested permission to come aboard. Jenna, eschewing military custom, jumped off the brow onto the ship ahead of me. There was a crowd waiting, sailors in red ball caps craning to get a look at Jenna. In fact, the crew would continue wearing red caps until the ship was decommissioned in 2015. Work on the pier stopped as crews from nearby ships craned their necks to see what the commotion was about.

It was a lot to take in, my old ship with new faces. So many years removed, so much life having drifted by in the currents of time. Jenna tugged at the leash, anxious to do what? Surely her nose must have been similarly overloaded, catching familiar smells of the ship that had been home for half of her life but not finding any former shipmates.

We were escorted to the wardroom, Jenna's old hangout and the scene of some of her greatest triumphs and worst embarrassments. From loosing her bowels during a gun shoot to wooing the chief of the Navy's wife, this room had been at the center of her—and my— lives during our tours. The place was packed as I had never seen it, at least thirty-five people crammed into the room. More than had been there to greet the CNO. When Jenna entered, it was as if a rock star had arrived, everyone working for an angle to see and pet her.

Jenna was a legend.

Commanding Officers come and go, your name forever engraved on a plaque outside of the captain's cabin. Jenna's mystique lived on not due to position but because of what she had done for the ship and crew. She remained a symbol of *Vandy* pride all these years later, not a hero like General Vandegrift, but something that set this ship apart from all others.

The master chief took Jenna around the ship to meet and greet the rest of the crew. Sailor after sailor stopped to pet her, each smiling broadly, each becoming a small part of her history. Carrying her up the ladders to the bridge, I noticed that we were getting a little older; I was not quite as spry springing up the steep ladders, and Jenna weighed a few pounds more. After I put her down on the deck, she turned and looked me in the eye, then walked out to the starboard bridge wing. I found her sitting next to the captain's chair, looking across the pier. But this time there were no flying fish. She got up and trotted a few yards aft and...squatted. The master chief chuckled as Jenna marked her spot for the last time. Linda looked horrified, but I smiled at her and shrugged my shoulders.

"At least she remembered to go up here instead of in a Pee-way."

When we got down to the mess decks, Jenna lifted her nose in the air. She went to her old corner, but there was no longer a bed of old blankets. Then she sniffed around the perimeter, looking into the faces and hands of the sailors in the room. No food was sliding off trays today. As we took her back to the wardroom, she pulled hard to port. Master chief let her lead, and we stepped out onto the smoke deck. Jenna looked around expectantly, but there were no sailors with handouts today.

Her tail sank, and she let master chief lead her back to the wardroom.

We had lunch at the same table where we debated getting a dog so many years before. The conversation was all about Jenna, answering the many whys, hows and wheres you have read about. Each story was eagerly consumed and provoked another batch of questions. More than one junior officer made a pointed remark about the benefits of having a dog on board, and I could tell from the captain's wry smile that he was getting pressure to reinvent Jenna. Several officers advocated that I should write a book, that this was a story that must not be lost. It was an idea that many shipmates had proposed, but I was not sure that I had the time.

As the ship rang the ceremonial bell for our departure, I felt a full range of emotions. Happiness at Jenna's tributes, sadness that our glory days were in our wake. I did not notice the industrial noises and smells of the pier, crossing the brow on autopilot without seeing my own steps. Knowing that we would never step foot on this ship again—Jenna's home and where I served my finest years in the Navy—was bittersweet. So many memories...of evading Chinese warships in Hong Kong... of being ordered to deep-six Jenna...of icy Korean winds and huge Pacific storms...of threats to shoot Jenna in Australia...of being "In the Navy" crossing the equator.

Of being part of a great crew, always ready to fight and win battles, always ready to party and win friends.

Of youth, confidence, camaraderie, and an unwavering belief in one another.

Of daily hardship, tedious watches, weekend duty days, and prolonged family separations.

Of a wedding on the fo'c'sle and burials at sea from the fantail, and every part of life in between.

We sailed this ship from California to Japan, west to Singapore, south to Australia, north to Korea, and east again to Hawaii. Rough seas, horizontal snow, Great Barrier Reef, Chinese Navy...nothing could stop us.

We were young and bold.

We were the *Vandy* Boyz *plus One*.

31.

TIME AND TIDE WAIT FOR NO ONE

Dogs' lives are too short. Their only fault, really.

— Agnes Sligh Turnbull

Jenna was approaching her final port of call. Although gimpy at the ripe age of sixteen, she still got around on her own. She scorned proffered help like a crotchety human senior citizen, maintaining her staunch independence. She did have ailments that came with being one hundred years old in human years. Her sight was dimmed despite surgery by an ophthalmologist. She no longer scarfed her food and had lost a few pounds, but if Linda was cooking something tasty, Jenna was soon at her feet no matter how soundly she had been sleeping in the back bedroom. Nose to floor like a bloodhound, she conducted kitchen patrol to ensure that no tender morsel went uneaten.

But even this salty sea dog could not stop time or tide, those irresistible forces that demarcate the earth. She had always waited for no one, seizing every opportunity to conduct unauthorized excursions whenever she could. Now, Jenna explored her yard during the day, went for shortening walks on the beach, and then relished a snack or two. Or three. She no longer got up to flank speed to escape the yard and go AWOL. Jenna was finally content, or resigned, to be a stay-at-home dog.

To our surprise, Jenna displayed powers that we were unaware of. It was not until after she retired that we uncovered her ability to foretell the future. When Linda and I faced a tough life decision that had multiple options, we turned to Jenna. Don't laugh! I wrote choices on pieces of paper, wadded them up, and spaced them equally on the floor. I ensured each was the same size, same color, and same odor. Jenna entered the room, saw the paper wads and headed over to investigate. She nosed one of the choices (which we counted as her selection), saw it wasn't edible, and instantly lost interest. We did this several times to determine which houses or lot to buy (twice), which contractor to do a major remodel (twice), and where to go on vacation. Each time we took her advice.

I see your skeptical look, and I don't blame you. Some of you are questioning our sanity, putting our financial well-being into the paws of a dog. As the captain of a ship, I had made thousands of decisions, some life changing, so why use a Shiba crystal ball? I don't have a rational answer. We employed Jenna when there was either no clear answer, or we were leaning in opposite directions. You may think that we gave her a clue as to which paper to pick, some sort of tell. Maybe, but I am an analyst and skeptic myself. We mixed the papers up so *we* had no clue which was which. Sometimes Jenna didn't pick our favored alternative, and then we would change some of the alternatives and try again. She would choose the same option.

We adhered to the furry seer's choices, and with 20/20 hindsight she was always correct.

Regrettably, I did not leverage her gift to make Super Bowl wagers.

We hosted a Sweet Sixteen birthday party for Jenna, unsure if our girl would last another year. Many of the old *Vandy* crew traveled to San Diego to celebrate Jenna's birthday and to reminisce about our salty times together. To see Jenna one last time. We were older, grayer, a bit wrinkled, and moved more deliberately, yet we still saw each other as we once were. Despite my protests, I was still the "Captain." It filled me with pride that I had once led this group, that I had some part in our momentous accomplishments and their individual successes. It was a great evening of rehashing old tales while watching white-sailed boats cross the blue-gray bay.

Wives rolled their eyes and sought another glass of wine as we chronicled story after story, reliving our youthful days on *Vandy* and reaffirming the bond that still held us together twelve years later. And celebrating our remarkable maritime saga in the company of our furry shipmate.

Jenna nosed around, not the perfect host but attentive to anyone who was eating. The only thing missing was birthday balloons. She still had PTSD from those shipboard gun shoots so many years before, and a popped balloon would make her shiver for hours. As she slowly made the circuit, each shipmate knelt and gently offered his hand. Jenna, eyes milky and muzzle frosty, sniffed each deeply. She looked up at each old shipmate, pausing for a minute, then continued her rounds. Was her only interest in procuring a handout, much like her many visits to the *Vandy* smoke deck? Or was she remembering this person? Did his scent bring her back to the old days, like this gathering had done for me? The fact that she visited each shipmate made me believe that she too was reliving the *Vandy* days.

After an hour she retired to her bed in the back bedroom. She had seen enough and gotten few handouts due to my strong oversight, as her stomach now could only handle specialized food. After many hours of sea stories, it was time for the grand finale. Jenna was not-so-softly snoring on her waterbed in the back, so we let her be. We couldn't trust her to blow out the candles anyway.

The sun had set, and the sky was transitioning from blue to gray to black. We lit the candles on the cake, and just as we started singing "Happy Birthday," Jenna gingerly made her grand entrance to delighted applause and laughter. We finished the song, and everyone took turns hugging and petting her. That was not her favorite part of the evening, but she endured it. Linda had bought special treats, and Jenna finally got goodies from the partygoers.

It was pitch-dark by the time the party broke up, everyone hesitant to leave. We had no idea what the future held, but we could always replay our good times when together. Our triumphs and exploits on the *Vandy* grew bigger and better, became sweeter as time passed, and bygone setbacks faded like a ship in the Hong Kong fog.

We knew this was Jenna's last *Vandy* engagement, her closing salutation. Each shipmate knelt for a final farewell, gently petting Jenna and attempting to keep his emotions in check. The mood, so luminous as we celebrated our special camaraderie, lost brilliance as we acknowledged Jenna's inexorable sunset.

32.

TAPS

Taps, taps, lights out.
Maintain silence about the decks.

— Nightly announcement on Navy ships

J enna lost her sea legs.

She could barely stand and tipped over if someone wasn't there to catch her. She complained despite a double dose of pain medication and anti-anxiety pills. She had always been stoic, the stereotypical inscrutable Asian, so when she cried while lying on her waterbed, we knew that she was in real distress. She was confused, spindly-legged, no longer the sure-footed sailor but now staggering into walls as if in heavy seas. But she still let us know when she had to go outside, needing some help to gain her legs and then lurching to the door. She had stopped eating two days earlier and had not had a bowel movement since then. We tried turkey, broth, chicken, salmon, beef tips, and treats.

She would not be tempted, an ominous sign for this former street urchin.

We all face death. Death of friends, family, and ourselves. But it is different when pets die. They do not fill out a living will or a form detailing how to care for them at the end. How can we even be sure they are at "the end"? People can relay their pain level on a scale of one to ten, but a pet cannot. We love and know our furry companions, we often know what they want and when something is wrong, but it is hard to know when to let them go. Humans usually choose life, even in the face of severe pain and hardship, withstanding chemotherapy, open-heart surgery, radical drugs, and radiation. But without verbal communication, we could not compare Jenna's level of pain to her will to live on, making it difficult to determine whether to keep fighting or to give up the ship.

Linda and I stood the dog watch on Jenna's final day. We pampered her and offered favorite treats, but nothing comforted or interested her. She lay stomach-down on her beloved waterbed, head on paws, staring vacantly. Waiting. We took turns lying beside her and trying to slow relentless time, trying to soothe her unrelenting pain. The hard-hearted clocks raced ahead, each minute more precious than the last.

We could not grasp that in just a few hours we would have her put down, that after today we would not see her again. Her curved smile and the sound of her nails clicking on the tile would never again warm our hearts. Contemplating her impending demise was even more difficult because she still looked good. Her red hair was full and glossy, her rabbit-down toes that Linda adored still bushy, her tail and feathers still luxuriant and full. Her triangular ears remained pointed upward, yet heard nothing. Her dark eyes stared ahead, yet remained vacant.

How could she be dying?

Jenna shivered and jerked her head at times, some unknown nerve setting off an involuntary reaction. She looked at me without expression when I tried to help her stand, so I lifted and turned her to ensure one side did not get sore.

We could not stop ourselves from glancing at the clock.

3:30...

4:00...

4:30...less than an hour until we had to get underway.

4:45...Linda laid beside her, stroking her face and promising a time ahead without pain. Jenna lay passive. I loaded her furry bed into the car for her final deployment.

I slowly returned to our bathroom—her den—and knelt down as tears blurred my vision. "I love you," I said, my voice quivering. "You have been the best dog and Navy mascot ever." I slid my hands under her and easily picked her up, her brittle ribs showing through her diminished frame. Jenna remained stock-still, legs straight out, no resistance, the antithesis of our feisty companion. I carried her past the stairs that had been her nemesis, past the kitchen where she had solicited daily for human chow. Out the front door for the last time. I laid her down in the car, and she lay motionless staring at me from her bed. This was not the warrior princess I knew, the fierce soul who demanded independence, the world traveler whose antics had tested Pakistan and won over the Chinese Navy.

Linda sat in the back seat beside Jenna. We were ready to go.

But we were not ready, we could never be ready to lose our beloved dog and shipmate. We were numb, trying to prolong every precious second.

Were we doing the right thing? Should we keep her alive? Maybe she would make a miraculous recovery.

How could we end her life without her concurrence, without Jenna telling us what she wanted?

But she was beyond that, beyond even complaining about the pain that wracked her body.

Time and Tide wait for no one.

Horns sounded behind us as we drove. I ignored them, for once not in a hurry to get to our destination. Linda had Jenna's head in her lap and was softly cooing while stroking her face, but there was no reaction. Even an open window, tempting new smells on every waft of air, could not induce a nose twitch.

Our tears flowed freely when we got to the vet, though we both detest emotional public displays. We were as mute as the pets in the reception area, unable through trembling jaws to mumble even a greeting or our name to the receptionist. She understood—they had done this before—and led us to a room. Neither of us had dealt with the death of a loved one, shielded by circumstance, timing, and parents.

I carried Jenna into the room, which was painted a soothing salmon color, with a shiny metal table in the middle. We had brought her furry bed so she could spend her last minutes lying in something familiar.

How did this lethal process work? I'm sure they had told me, but my brain was functioning about as well as my mouth.

Would it take long? My mind conjured the chair where they inject and kill death row prisoners.

Would there be pain?

There was pain now. Jenna was in pain, and so were we.

The veterinarian and her team had always treated Jenna like a queen, and they were empathetic and unhurried. An aide gently lifted Jenna and took her away, then brought her back a few minutes later with a catheter in her front right leg. The bright pink bandage covering the catheter where the "medicine" would be injected failed to cheer us. The vet entered and explained that she would give Jenna a sedative to put her to sleep, and then an injection to stop her heart.

The end was at hand.

It was surreal, time and space adrift in an unseen current, at once physically holding Jenna yet feeling her being pulled from my grasp. I had been in that room many times, but now the walls seemed too close, the bright colors not cheerful. The doctor told us to call her when we were ready, then gently closed the door as she left.

And then it happened.

Jenna let us know that she was ready.

From somewhere deep inside, she loosed a prolonged, wavering yowl. We hugged and stroked her, murmuring soft words, but she continued to moan and weakly struggle. I didn't know if it was pain or something misfiring in her brain, but she had reached her limit.

Like a good sailor, she was reporting that she was ready to *go ashore* for the last time.

I picked her up and cradled her on my lap, which quieted her. I looked into her eyes, once so brilliant and alive with mischief but now unblinking and unfocused. The doctor returned with syringes in hand. She was sympathetic and very pregnant. Life follows death. We had not discussed how to position Jenna, so I left her in my lap. Linda sat to my left and caressed Jenna's head.

We were ready.

We would never be ready, but it had to be done. Jenna was in pain, and we couldn't stand her suffering. She was curled up, barely moving. I put my hand under her chest and felt her heart beating. We nodded to the doctor, too choked up to utter a sound.

She gave Jenna the tranquilizer.

Jenna relaxed and was still. I couldn't tell whether she was asleep, but the doctor said she was.

The doctor gave Jenna the heart-stopping medicine, and her head drooped.

I could no longer feel her heartbeat, and I was certain that mine had stopped as well.

We were crying inconsolably, desolate and unbelieving and in shock. Jenna looked so natural; her eyes open, her ears so soft. Her legs unwound, the pain of arthritis gone. I gently stroked her face, and her jaw quivered.

I knew it was nerves reacting involuntarily, but I still peered into her eyes with hope. They were blank and unmoving.

I couldn't feel her heart anymore. I couldn't feel my heart anymore.

I carefully placed her on the table, our beautiful dog now a lifeless corpse. We kept looking at her, not believing that she was gone. How could this dog that had so much life and energy, this dog that inspired an entire ship for many years, be dead?

We lingered, petting her, looking into her eyes. It felt wrong to leave her here, to leave her with strangers, to leave her and never again see her. To never again walk through the neighborhood with her, to never again feed her, to never again pick up after her, to never again wash and comb her.

We tore ourselves away, watching her as we slowly backed from the room. Perhaps she would jump up, tongue wagging, tail curled over her back, ears at the ready.

No.

I don't remember the ride home. The house felt empty, its spirit gone, our dream retirement house—selected on a piece of paper by Jenna—now bland and lifeless. Too big for just the two of us.

The mesquite wood entranceway, brought from Texas, had no meaning except for the tiny scratches from her paws. Marble, travertine, stainless steel, granite...archways and high ceilings...a panoramic view of San Diego harbor, the Pacific Ocean, and the hills of Mexico beyond...all meaningless and trite.

Stuff.

The love and life we had just lost were priceless and irreplaceable.

We cried as we looked at her stuff. I took her beds, towels, bowls, and other accoutrements out to the garage. We could not look at them, the pain too raw, our grieving so sharp. I told myself she was *just a dog*, but that didn't work.

She was an important part of our lives.

She made us happy, and we gave her the best life that we could.

It was a long night, with more tears than sleep. We went to bed early, unable to watch TV. Even its mindless chatter could not disconnect our minds from reality. Our bathroom was so much bigger without her bed and bowls. So sterile and cold without her.

I knew that Jenna was in a better place, but I wondered about her precious body. Where was it? Had it been gently taken care of, or roughly handled by someone hardened to those duties. I tossed and turned, picturing her being lugged away in a black plastic garbage bag.

We received her remains after cremation, perhaps for some future ceremony with her crew, perhaps even to be held on the *Vandegrift*. They had replicated her paw prints in ceramic, and I realized that those prints were made with her cold, stiffening paws.

I didn't like to look at them.

Someday, but not yet.

The next day my sadness swelled, preventing any ability to read or absorb TV. There seemed to be no color in the world; smells and tastes were flat and bland. The clock took two clicks forward, then one click back.

A day without Jenna finally ended.

I understood that time would heal, and I would eventually enjoy the pleasures of life. That I would see the world in jumbled shades of gray for only so long, and then one day color and life would bloom again. That we would enjoy life.

But...

That seemed like a theory provided by scientists without feelings, or a feel-good Hallmark card.

As we lay in bed, sleepless, the floor creaked. We reflexively started to jump up, thinking it was Jenna. We heard her often, a neighborhood dog barking or some household noise replicating one of her sounds. Or did we hear these echoes because we wanted to? We yearned to pet her, to see her foxy face.

To watch her rise one last time, stretch while rolling her tongue out like a carpet, and with a quick shake set out on her next adventure.

STAY DAWN

Stay Dawn
slow your wings
that speed toward me
this night

Hold back the Sun
racing across longitudes
eager for a splashy entrance
on eastern stage

Let Night
keep her black shawl
brightening moon and stars
a while longer

Slow the incoming Tide
eternal and relentless
allow me more Time
to prepare

Morning reveille
of bright birdsong
brings no joy or hope
of happiness

For this Day
sails in under gathering clouds
bringing ending and grief
along this shore

Red skies at morn
do this day warn
a shipmate will not see
Night's return.

Neal Kusumoto
Feb. 5, 2013
For Jenna

EPILOGUE

*Any man who may be asked in this century
what he did to make his life worthwhile,
I think can respond with a good
deal of pride and satisfaction:
"I served in the United States Navy."*

— PRESIDENT JOHN F. KENNEDY

We can finally gaze at Jenna's picture on the mantel next to her urn. We pet the frame sometimes as we say goodnight, as if she lives on and will materialize and yawn, lazily rolling out her tongue and stretching her legs out, all the while eyeing us to ascertain what's next. Every once in a while, something hits a raw nerve and tears pop into my eyes. We look at her ceramic paw prints and caress them as if to touch her toes, but they are cold and hard, not the downy-soft warm toes we yearn for. But they somehow still exude her essence, like a candle's scent brings forth a mental snapshot of a pine tree. We have yet to open the small wood "coffin" with her ashes inside, still cannot contemplate spreading them and losing her once more.

We don't get around the neighborhood as much, but we take Jenna's route when we do take walks. We can't help from commenting, "This was her favorite lawn" or, "She would have liked to meet that dog." On walks, Jenna always wanted to know what had gone on since her last visit, who had left a calling card, no doubt appreciating their last meal through her keen nose. If the bouquet was particularly good, she'd brace her legs, ready to resist any tug on the leash until she had inhaled every last scent-video left behind. No wonder she had looked forward to her walk every day; it was her chance to smell what was happening in her world.

A few weeks after Jenna's death, we saw a dog that looked like her, only without pointy bat ears. It was red, about the same size, waiting for its owner. We do this often, considering each dog we see and comparing them to Jenna.

They never measure up.

Our backyard lawn is recovering, and there are no longer dog-down tumbleweeds rolling about the house. Much cleaner and neater, but flat and lifeless. This was Jenna's yard, her own private space in the world. She never tired of checking out the perimeter, sniffing out comings and goings invisible to us. These outings were her entertainment and communications network, acting as her TV, internet, and telephone. Where we saw a visual palette of flowers, she accessed a much more vibrant World Wide Web via her nose-net.

We seldom venture into the backyard now, don't even water it. Jenna would be disheartened to find that skunks now boldly traverse her territory as they make their nightly hunting trek into the valley below. That never happened while she was here, and I am sorry that we have not maintained a taut watch. Jenna left a big gap in our lives, a hole that remains unfilled.

I stand in Jenna's yard and gaze down the San Diego channel, beyond the red and green buoys to the Pacific Ocean. A light breeze roughens the water to a sandpaper texture, creating a blue-green mosaic that ripples in the fading light. The setting sun's rays wrap around the earth, accentuating its curvature. The rounded orange edge burns bright against the cool purple sky, a glowing ring surrounded by a diffused golden fog. Slowly cooling, growing dark, the golden orb relinquishes its hold as it sinks beneath the horizon. Colors fade, the world is sepia-toned in purple hues...then becomes black and white...and then just black. I spot Sirius, the Dog Star that followed us across so many seas, blinking from across the celestial heavens. The harbor, waves, and rocky promontory vanish under a dark cloak, and in my blindness the ocean sounds are amplified.

As the fog of time thickens, I look back in wonder at our impetuous actions and bulletproof attitude as we sailed across the seas. Jenna strolling into the wardroom and brushing past a startled Chief of the Navy to put her paws in his wife's lap replays slowly in my mind's eye. *Fortune Favored Our Boldness*. As I rock on my heels, I can hear the *Vandy*'s bow cutting through the sea—a continuous hiss like an untuned radio—and feel the gentle rocking as the ship slides through tranquil seas. I overhear the reports of the bridge watch as they steer the ship, the watch standers enjoying the short dog watch before dinner. Even now I can see a red foxy dog staring at me from the top of the ladder, head high and ears alert...oblivious to her place in Navy history and in our hearts.

FRIGATE CHARACTERISTICS

USS *Vandegrift* (FFG-48) was an Oliver Hazard Perry-class frigate of the United States Navy. The ship was named for General Alexander A. Vandegrift (1887–1973), eighteenth Commandant of the Marine Corps and hero of the Battle of Guadalcanal.

Oliver Hazard Perry-class frigates were designed as anti-aircraft and anti-submarine warfare guided-missile warships intended to provide open-ocean escort of amphibious warfare ships and merchant ship convoys in moderate threat environments in a potential war with the Soviet Union and the Warsaw Pact countries. They could also provide air defense against 1970s- and 1980s-era aircraft and anti-ship missiles. These warships were equipped to escort and protect aircraft carrier battle groups, amphibious landing groups, underway replenishment groups, and merchant ship convoys. They conducted independent operations to perform such tasks as surveillance of illegal drug smugglers, maritime interception operations, and exercises with other nations.

- Displacement: 4,100 long tons
- Length: 445 feet

- Beam: 45 feet
- Draft: 22 feet
- Propulsion: 2 × General Electric LM2500-30 gas turbines generating 41,000 horsepower
- Speed: 29+ knots
- Range: 4,500 nautical miles at 20 knots
- Radar: AN/SPS-49 and AN/SPS-55 for air and surface search
- Sonar: SQS-56, SQR-19 Towed Array for submarine detection
- MK-13 missile launcher with a 40-missile magazine containing SM-1MR anti-aircraft guided missiles and Harpoon anti-ship missiles
- Six anti-submarine warfare torpedo tubes with Mark 46 torpedoes
- Oto Melara 76 mm/62 caliber naval gun
- 20 mm Phalanx CIWS rapid-fire cannon
- Two LAMPS multi-purpose helicopters
- Complement: 20 officers, 20 chief petty officers, and 185 enlisted

— Unclassified information from Wikipedia

NOTES

1. Name changed.
2. This is a nondenominational, nonsexist book that uses "he" in a generic manner.
3. For those of you on Wikipedia, I know there are not really seven "seas."
4. Name changed to protect the guilty.
5. General Vandegrift's granddaughter asserted that John was not related to the general during a conversation at USS Vandegrift's decommissioning. It is difficult to believe that he was lying.
6. Sake is often consumed from small wooden box cups at ceremonies.
7. RAND Corporation study, 2013.

ACKNOWLEDGMENTS

Special thanks to those who made this book possible.

Linda Kusumoto (wife, editor, and motivator)
Rita Rosenkranz (agent)
Diane O'Connell
Heather Ashby Nickodem
John Vandegrift
Valerie Ormond Navarro
Kelli Coy (photographer)
Jerry Ferguson (Captain, US Navy ret)
Lynn McDaniel
Post Hill Press
Military Writers Society of America